The Great Financial Plumbing

The Great Financial Plumbing

From Northern Rock to Banking Union

Karel Lannoo

**Foreword
by Danuta Hübner**

Centre for European Policy Studies (CEPS), Brussels
Rowman & Littlefield International, London

Published by Rowman & Littlefield International, Ltd.
Unit A, Whitacre Mews, 26-34 Stannary Street, London SE11 4AB
www.rowmaninternational.com

Rowman & Littlefield International Ltd. is an affiliate of Rowman & Littlefield
4501 Forbes Boulevard, Suite 200, Lanham, Maryland 20706, USA
With additional offices in Boulder, New York, Toronto (Canada) and Plymouth (UK)
www.rowman.com

Copyright © 2015 Centre for European Policy Studies

Centre for European Policy Studies
Place du Congrès 1, B-1000 Brussels
Tel: (32.2) 229.39.11 Fax: (32.2) 219.41.51
E-mail: info@ceps.eu
Website: http://www.ceps.eu

British Library Cataloguing in Publication Data
A catalogue record for this book is available from the British Library

ISBN: 978-1-78348-428-7

⊖™ The paper used in this publication meets the minimum requirements of American National Standard for Information Sciences—Permanence of Paper for Printed Library Materials, ANSI/NISO Z39.48-1992.

Printed in the United States of America

TABLE OF CONTENTS

LIST OF FIGURES, TABLES AND BOXES

LIST OF ABBREVIATIONS

ABS	asset-backed securities
AIFMD	alternative investment fund managers Directive
AuM	assets under management
AQR	asset quality review
BCBS	Basel Committee on Banking Supervision
BIS	Bank for International Settlements
BRRD	bank recovery and resolution Directive
BU	Banking Union
CCP	central counterparty
CDO	collateralised debt obligation
CDS	credit default swap
CEBS	Committee of European Banking Supervisors
CEIOPS	Committee of European Insurance and Occupational Pensions Supervisors
CEREP	central repository
CESR	Committee of European Securities Regulators
CET1	Common Equity Tier 1 capital
CFTC	Commodity Futures Trading Commission
CJEU	Court of Justice of the European Union
CPMI	Committee on Payments and Market Infrastructures
CRA	credit rating agency
CRD	capital requirements Directive
CRR	capital requirements Regulation
CSD	central securities depository
CSDR	central securities depository Regulation
DGS	deposit guarantee schemes
EBA	European Banking Authority
ECAI	External Credit Assessment Institution
ECB	European Central Bank
EEA	European Economic Area
EFC	Economic and Financial Committee
EFSF	European Financial Stability Facility
EIOPA	European Insurance and Occupational Pensions Authority
ELA	emergency liquidity assistance
ELTIFs	European long-term investment funds

EMIR	European market infrastructure Regulation
ESAs	European Supervisory Authorities
ESCB	European System of Central Banks
ESFS	European System of Financial Supervisors
ESM	European Stability Mechanism
ESMA	European Securities and Markets Authority
ESRB	European Systemic Risk Board
ETD	exchange-traded derivative
FINREP	financial reporting (for supervisory purposes)
FMI	financial market infrastructure
FMUs	financial market utilities
FSA	Financial Services Authority
FSAP	Financial Services Action Plan
FSB	Financial Stability Board
FSOC	Financial Services Oversight Council
G-20	Group of Twenty
G-SIBs	global systemically important banks
G-SII	global systemically important institution
GAAP	generally accepted accounting principles
HQLA	high-quality liquid assets
IFRS	International Financial Reporting Standards
IORP	Institution for Occupational Retirement Provision
IOSCO	International Organisation of Securities Commissions
IRB	internal ratings-based (approach)
ISDA	International Swaps and Derivatives Association
ITS	implementing technical standard
JST	joint supervisory team
KID	key information document
KIID	key investor information document
LCR	liquidity coverage ratio
MAD	market abuse Directive
MAR	market abuse Regulation
MBS	mortgage-backed securities
MiFID	markets in financial instruments Directive
MiFIR	markets in financial instruments Regulation
MMF	money market fund
MPOE	multiple point of entry
MREL	minimum requirement for own funds and eligible liabilities

NAV	net asset value
NCA	nationally competent authority
NRSRO	nationally recognized statistical rating organization
NSFR	net stable funding ratio
OMT	outright monetary transaction
O-SII	other systemically important institution
OTC	over-the-counter
PRIIP	packaged retail and insurance-linked investment product
PRIP	packaged retail investment product
REFIT	Regulatory Fitness and Performance Programme
RMBS	residential mortgage-backed securities
RTS	regulatory technical standard
RW	risk weight
SEC	Securities and Exchange Commission
SIFI	systemically important financial institution
SME	small- and medium-sized enterprise
S&P	Standard & Poor's
SPOE	single point of entry
SRA	Single Resolution Authority
SRB	Single Resolution Board
SRB	standardised ratings-based (approach)
SRM	Single Resolution Mechanism
T2S	Target 2 Securities
TARP	Troubled Asset Relief Program
TER	total expense ratio
UCITS	Undertakings for Collective Investments in Transferable Securities

FOREWORD

The past few years have been a crucial period for financial regulation in Europe: lessons have been drawn from the major gaps and failures that had led to the 2008-09 crisis and dramatic changes have taken place in almost all areas related to financial services.

The sheer scale of the work that has been done to tighten financial regulation in the EU is undeniably impressive. With regard to this aspect of legislation, many steps have been taken towards making our financial system more stable and resilient. However, the jury is still out concerning the ability of this reformed financial system to deliver on growth. Now that we are a few years into the implementation of some of the earlier measures, it is time to take a step back, take stock of the changes introduced and identify the improvements that can be made.

In a context in which many decisions have been taken in a short timeframe, timely, proper and effective implementation of the measures agreed on is also of the essence and should be, in the near future, one of the main priorities. In some cases, it is only when full implementation is effective that it will be possible to assess whether the objectives of the legislation have been met. For instance, one of the objectives of the wave of financial re-regulation was to eliminate the moral-hazard problems caused by institutions that were considered too-big-to-fail. The moving of supervision to a higher decision level, intended, inter alia, to limit the possible leniency of national supervisors towards their own institutions, as well as the re-design of the insolvency architecture with the introduction of tools such as bail-in and the establishment of a single resolution fund, were intended to achieve this goal.

The new system is to be gradually implemented over time, however, and it might still be too early to judge whether the provisions will be sufficient. In the same vein, it is not at all clear whether the Banking Union in its current shape has really managed in practice to break the negative bank-sovereign feedback loop, which was its original aim.

Of course, beyond the effort made in terms of financial re-regulation, the current situation in the EU is raising other issues and calling for action in different fields. A case in point is the need to promote growth and investment, for which the need is pressing but which, so far, has been eclipsed by the necessity to amend the regulatory framework. It is time, now that timid growth seems to be returning and the bulk of the work in terms of financial regulation has been done, to shift our focus to innovation and investment. Welcome initiatives to this end have been taken or reflected on at the EU level. In particular, the Capital Markets Union project aims at decreasing to some extent the reliance on bank funding, which has for years been a fixture on the EU's financial landscape, in order to provide new, alternative sources of funding for European companies and thereby bridge some of the investment gap that we have been witnessing for years. This issue of investment will surely be one of the major topics of discussion for years to come.

Two final issues raised by the progress made towards a tightening of financial regulation are the democratic accountability of the system and the divide between the members and the non-members of the eurozone.

One of the ways to address the first issue, which has been pending for some time and has been brought to the fore by the increase in EU competences that accompanied the recent reforms, should be to strengthen the role of the European Parliament but also of national parliaments in the decision-making and monitoring processes. The process of monetary dialogue with the European Central Bank and the conclusion of interinstitutional agreements between the European Parliament on the one side and, respectively, the ECB carrying out its tasks within the framework of the Single Supervisory Mechanism and, soon, the Single Resolution Board, on the other side, are mechanisms that can be built on. But the crucial role of national parliaments should be taken into account and a way of involving them more closely should be reflected on.

The recent developments relating to the Banking Union also entail the risk of increased fragmentation and of a divide between countries that are members of the euro area and therefore de facto members of the Banking Union, and the others that have to choose to opt in. Bearing in mind that most of the countries that are currently not members of the euro area are actually pre-ins, i.e. they intend to adopt the single currency once they meet the criteria, there is a solid case for a system that allows non-euro area countries to remain as closely involved as possible in the decisions taken in the euro area. This should be kept in mind in a context in which there is sometimes a tendency to push for a reinforcement of the cohesion of the 'core' in order to solve immediate issues and demonstrate credibility in the short term. A balance must be found and the issue of multi-speed Europe is certainly one of the most important current constitutional questions to explore.

As a contribution to the effort to evaluate and take stock of recently-passed legislation in order to identify and address future issues, this book is a welcome body of work and a very useful background document.

Danuta Hübner
Member of the European Parliament

PREFACE

The financial crisis has led to a far-reaching redesign of the European regulatory and supervisory framework. Following the commitments made in the context of discussions in the G-20, but also reacting to internal shortcomings, the EU engaged in a massive programme to re-regulate financial institutions and markets. The EU furthermore redesigned the structure for supervisory cooperation, initially through the European Supervisory Authorities, and later with Banking Union.

The purpose of this book is to systematically assess the new regulatory and supervisory framework. Its structure reflects the big items on the agenda: 1) better supervisory cooperation and integration; 2) the G-20 items: better oversight of credit rating agencies, improved capital standards for banks, a larger role for central clearing in derivative markets and the regulation of alternative investment funds, depositor protection and bank liquidation rules; and 3) specific EU matters, namely state aid, which acted as a surrogate for harmonised bank resolution.

This book aims to give professionals, students and policy-makers a better understanding of the new regulatory framework and of the policy context that has led to the new rules. The intention is not to discuss the causes of the crisis from a European perspective, although this is certainly done in the various chapters, especially in the introductory chapter. The Annex provides an overview of the different pieces of regulation and the businesses to which they apply.

CEPS has built up considerable expertise in the regulation and integration of financial markets in its 30-plus years of operations, of which this book is the result and the beneficiary. I would like to thank the numerous colleagues who helped me in preparing the various chapters and without whom it would have been impossible to finalise this book.

In particular, I wish to acknowledge the valuable research assistance and input provided by my colleagues Cosmina Amariei, Willem Pieter De Groen, Jan-Martin Frie, Mirzha de Manuel Aramendía and Diego Valiante. I am also grateful for many discussions with CEPS Corporate Members and other stakeholders, which yielded useful insights. Finally, I wish to thank Anne Harrington and Lee Gillette for patiently editing the text, Els Van den Broeck for skilfully formatting the entire draft and my sister Wiennie for designing the cover.

I am delighted that the results of this collective effort can be made available to a broader readership.

Karel Lannoo
Chief Executive Officer, CEPS
Brussels

1. THE POLICY REACTION TO THE CRISIS: A MOVING TARGET

This is not just another volume about the causes or the history of the financial crisis. Rather, it is a book about the actions taken by the European Union to prevent a crisis of this magnitude from ever erupting again. A far-reaching redesign of the European regulatory and supervisory framework was undertaken, following the commitments the EU made in the context of discussions in the G-20 summit meetings[1] and in reaction to serious internal shortcomings. The creation of a Banking Union (BU) with the shift of banking supervision from national authorities to the European Central Bank (ECB), at least for the eurozone, and the creation of a Single Resolution Board (SRB) have been the most tangible outcomes.

This book aims to systematically discuss and assess the new regulatory and supervisory framework in a readable and accessible way. The structure follows the big themes on the agenda: What is changing with Banking Union? Have the G-20 concerns been adequately addressed by the EU: oversight of credit rating agencies, better and more capital for banks, the re-regulation of securities and derivatives markets, asset management, depositor protection and bank resolution? And how were uniquely EU rules on the prohibition of state aid applied to the banking sector during the crisis?

Although much has been done at the global, regional and national level, this book concentrates on the response taken directly

---

[1] The G-20 (or Group of 20) Summit was created as a response both to the financial crisis of 2008–10 and to a growing recognition that key emerging countries were not adequately represented in the core of global economic discussions and governance. For an appraisal of the G-20's efforts to develop a more sustainable regulatory framework for financial institutions, see Lannoo (2014).

by the EU to the financial crisis. Some EU member states in particular, spurred on by their electorates, have taken action, but not necessarily in coordination with entities at the EU level. Attention is paid, however, when the response by EU member states has contravened EU rules, most importantly regarding those governing state aid to the banks. This book does not discuss the EU's reaction to the economic crisis, although both crises ran in parallel, at least from 2010 onwards, as the worsening of the fiscal situation of the sovereigns affected the domestic banking sectors in the distressed countries and led to the formation of Banking Union.

This book presents seven different themes of re-regulation and new supervisory structures, in line with issues dominating the global and European agenda. Action on these items has not necessarily been coordinated. A political consensus grew at different stages during the crisis that action was necessary. Some policy actions even pre-date the financial crisis, such as the efforts to regulate rating agents. Other elements came very late, such as recognition of the need to transfer supervision to the ECB, as it became clear that the level of supervisory cooperation created with the European Supervisory Authorities (ESAs)[2] was insufficient to deal with the problems in the European banking sector. But the different themes are sequenced chronologically, in the same order as they emerged during the crisis.

Seen in hindsight, much was achieved at EU level over a period of about seven years. From the early days, in the second half of 2007 to June 2012, when agreement was reached on transferring banking supervision to the ECB, and to early 2014, when agreements were reached on the EU's bank recovery and resolution Directive (BRRD) and the Single Resolution Mechanism (SRM). No less than 38 different actions in the area of financial reform were proposed by the European Commission during that period, most of

---

[2] As early as September 2009, the European Commission brought forward proposals to replace the EU's existing supervisory architecture with a European system of financial supervisors (ESFS), consisting of three European Supervisory Authorities (ESAs) – a European Banking Authority (EBA), a European Securities and Markets Authority (ESMA) and a European Insurance and Occupational Pensions Authority (EIOPA). The three ESAs and a European Systemic Risk Board (ESRB) were established in January 2011 to replace the former supervisory committees.

which were completed by the end of 2014. These proposals entailed even more legislative actions, as often the particular financial reform was split over different legal instruments, a directive and a regulation, for example, or was further subdivided.

In the early days of the crisis, which was caused by growing risks and losses in the US subprime housing market, it rapidly became clear that the EU regulatory framework was inadequate and that supervisory cooperation was not as strong as it should have been, given the level of market integration. In certain domains, the reaction took time to materialise in concrete proposals, whereas in others, it crystallised rapidly. The bank run on Northern Rock in September 2007 – the first since Victorian times in Britain – emphasised that essential elements of the framework for managing a financial crisis simply did not work, and that the operational model and the level of harmonisation of the 1994 Directive on deposit guarantee schemes (DGS) were seriously flawed. But it was not until 2014 that agreement was finally reached on the need to implement real reform at EU level.

The failure of two local German banks in September 2007 revealed three major shortcomings: the absence of supervisory cooperation (or the presence of destructive regulatory competition in the EU), the deficiencies in the prudential rules covering securitisation and consolidation, and the lack of proper risk management in the banks. It brought about a consensus among EU member states on the need to insist on maximum harmonisation of rules and a fully identical set of financial rules, namely the 'single rulebook', and to improve supervisory cooperation and the functioning of the supervisory colleges of banks. The building blocks for an upgrade of the three Committees of Supervisors, the so-called 'Level-3 Committees' – the Committee of European Banking Supervisors (CEBS), the Committee of European Insurance and Occupational Pensions Supervisors (CEIOPS) and the Committee of European Securities Regulators (CESR) – were being put in place that would eventually equip them to become fully-fledged agencies. On the legislative side, agreement was reached in the early days of the crisis that rating agencies should be regulated at EU level and the treatment of securitisation in the first capital requirements Directive (CRD I) should be changed.

On the more systemic side, however, there was scant awareness among policy-makers in the first year of the crisis, leading up to the failure of Lehman Brothers, of the deep weaknesses in the EU financial system and in its oversight.[3] Against the background of mounting losses in the EU financial system, estimated at the time to amount to about €272 billion, no fundamental decisions were taken towards more centralised oversight. The finance ministers, meeting in the Ecofin Council, reacted by issuing a roadmap and increasing the level of tasks for the Level-3 Committees, but without upgrading their means or legal status. In its May 2008 meeting, the Council stressed in its conclusions: "The EU Committees of Supervisors should be able to gather aggregate information in order to assess these features within and across financial sectors and to alert the Economic and Financial Committee (EFC)[4] to potential and imminent threats in the financial system."

One may wonder, however, whether the Council fully appreciated the magnitude of the task it was assigning to the Level-3 Committees, each of which employed only about 15 persons. The Council also reacted with a new memorandum of understanding amongst the supervisory authorities, central banks and finance ministries to improve supervisory cooperation and the functioning of the Colleges. No less than 113(!) different EU authorities were signatories to the agreement. A more serious reaction, considering the staggering losses that were then mounting in the financial system, would have prepared the EU much better for confronting what was still to come.

The phase that started in September 2008 is well known, but many policy-makers continued to believe that the problem was caused by the US financial system. There was not only the failure of Lehman Brothers, but also the bail-out by the US Treasury of the insurance giant AIG and the growing problems in US monoline insurers. AIG alone received an emergency loan of $85 billion from the Federal Reserve of New York, $22.4 billion of which went to

---

[3] The following section draws from Lannoo (2008).

[4] Composed of senior officials from national administrations, central banks, the ECB and the European Commission, the Economic and Financial Committee (EFC) was established on the basis of the Maastricht Treaty to promote policy coordination among the member states.

banks, and more than half of the latter sum went to European banks in collateral relating to credit default swap (CDS) transactions from AIG. Its default would thus have meant even-deeper trouble for European banks.

The biggest shock for the banks in Europe came from the short-term lending market, which froze almost overnight. Banks with a large amount of short-term loans on their balance sheets, often related to takeovers or risky business models, were the first victims, such as Dexia or Fortis in Belgium. Lending costs jumped overnight. The crisis had become systemic, which forced EU governments to react. Ireland was the first country to guarantee liabilities in its banking system, forcing the UK and other EU countries to follow suit. The Dutch, British and French governments suggested the creation of a European banking resolution fund, but Germany was strongly opposed to such an idea. The country-by-country reactions and the existence of a variety of national bank guarantee and bail-out schemes led to deep distortions in the single market, which fundamentally changed the landscape of European banking. The overall level of the support, representing about 14% of GDP, helped EU countries to recover rapidly, but it also lay the ground for the ensuing sovereign crisis, by rapidly increasing government-debt levels and highlighting the differences in the quality of public finances.

The EU reacted by instituting the High-Level Expert Group on EU Financial Supervision, chaired by Jacques de Larosière, former Governor of the Bank of France. The de Larosière report proposed, inter alia, the creation of the European System of Financial Supervisors (ESFS), composed of the European Supervisory Authorities (ESAs) and the European Systemic Risk Board (ESRB), and called for a meeting of the G-20 at the level of heads of state and government. The latter convened first in Washington, D.C. in November 2008, and set the stage for a globally coordinated process of financial re-regulation in the successive London and Pittsburgh G-20 summits. The London G-20 agreed "to extend regulation and oversight to all systemically important financial institutions, instruments and markets…to take action, once recovery is assured, to improve the quality, quantity, and international consistency of capital in the banking system", to regulate rating agencies and hedge funds, and to ensure that "all standardized OTC derivative contracts should be traded on exchanges or electronic trading platforms, where appropriate, and cleared through central counterparties", and "to develop an international framework for cross-border bank resolution arrangements". The Financial Stability Board (FSB) within the G-20 was given the central role of leading this process.

The G-20 agenda was followed-up closely by EU policy-makers, and formed the background on which the majority of the proposals for regulatory reform were based. But it became rapidly clear that the institutional reform that was intended by the creation of the ESAs was not sufficient, above all for banking. The stress tests carried out by the European Banking Authority (EBA) did not succeed in calming fears about the state of the EU banking sector, as their results were in each case rapidly overtaken by events. The stress test of July 2010 – which had been carried out by EBA's predecessor (the CEBS) – concluded that an additional €3.5 billion capital was needed for about seven banks, five of which were Spanish. But by mid-August 2010, the moribund Anglo-Irish Bank, although it had not been included in the test, was in need of another transfusion of €10 billion and by September, it appeared that the capital needs of Spanish savings banks were much greater than originally foreseen. The 2011 stress test was followed by growing uncertainties about the capital needs of these Spanish banks, which were estimated to be around €60 billion, whereas the test had concluded that the minimum shortfall for eight banks in meeting a 5% core tier 1 ratio was about €2.5 billion. The deep uncertainties in European financial markets at that time led to a formal decision at the level of the heads of state and government in the October 2011 European Council to require EU banks to meet a 9% Tier 1 ratio by June 2012.

The sovereign crisis and the dreaded 'doom loop' created by the dependence of banks on the quality of the finances of their sovereign was the second element leading to the decision for deeper institutional reform, and the creation of a Banking Union. The wide differences in funding costs of banks risked derailing the single financial market, as the cost of credit to banks in the peripheral countries was much higher than in the North. This also risked undermining the single monetary policy.

The second report prepared under the leadership of Herman Van Rompuy (2012) and published ahead of the June 2012 European Council, proposed the creation of a Banking Union, to be composed of a single European banking supervision system, a European resolution and a European deposit insurance scheme. The European Council decided, barely two years after the start of the European Banking Authority, to move supervision to the ECB, based upon Art. 127(6) of the EU Treaty. Agreements on the deposit guarantee schemes Directive (DGSD) and the Single Resolution Mechanism (SRM) followed in early 2014, even if reaching agreement on the centralisation of the latter function at the eurozone level was problematic in view of the reach of the EU Treaty.

1.1 The book at a glance

Credit Rating Agencies: The early targets (chapter 2). From having virtually no rules, the EU moved with great alacrity to agree on regulation and centralised supervision of credit rating agencies (CRAs) in a matter of a few months. But the rules did not change the 'issuer-pays' model of rating agents and its inherent conflicts of interest. Five years after the Regulation on credit rating agencies came in force, the sector remains highly concentrated, with the Big 3 – Standard & Poor's (S&P), Moody's Investors Services and Fitch Ratings – controlling about 90% of the EU market. Also the regulatory reliance on ratings remains elevated, despite the ambition to reduce it, as both supervisors and monetary policy authorities continue to refer to ratings for policy purposes. A more fundamental change in the business model of rating agents could have avoided the detailed conflict-of-interest, transparency and competition provisions of the regulation.

Game Change in Asset Management (chapter 3). The asset management industry was more affected by the crisis than its representatives acknowledged. Not only did it solidify the view that the hedge fund industry should be regulated, but it also spilled over to other parts of the asset management industry, and more prudential and conduct-of-business regulation was adopted. The Ponzi scheme perpetrated by Bernard Madoff fell apart by the end of 2008, highlighting the lack of separation between depositories and managers. More conflict-of-interest and remuneration regulation followed in the wake of the overall debate over the distorted incentive structures found throughout the financial industry.

Solidifying Derivatives Markets and Financial Infrastructure (chapter 4). One of the hallmarks of the London and Pittsburgh G-20 summit meetings was the determination to require central clearing of OTC (over-the-counter) derivatives contracts, at least for the contracts that can be standardised. The result was a huge structural change, which a few years later brought the largest part of the OTC market into central clearing and trading. These changes, however, required detailed discussions on which products should be centrally cleared and even more on the prudential standards for central counterparties, which are still in the course of implementation.

New Capital Requirements: Basel III implementation in EU law (chapter 5). The element that attracted the most attention as a result of the crisis, namely the banks' lack of capital, required extensive discussions before agreement was reached on the new rules at international level, with the Basel III agreement in December 2010, and even more time to formulate the EU rules in the capital requirements Directive (CRD IV) in September 2013. In the meantime, some steps were taken with the addition of 'skin in the game' or retention requirements for securitisation in 2009, and the governance and remuneration amendments in 2010. The result at the end is a complete paradigm shift, with the larger the bank, the more capital it needs to amass, through additional capital buffer requirements. The only element advantaging large banks that has not been changed so far are the internal models to calculate the capital at risk. Basel III and the CRD IV also set rules for the minimum level of liquidity for banks, for the first time at international and EU level.

The ECB as Bank Supervisor (chapter 6). The biggest institutional change as a result of the crisis was the agreement, taken by consensus by all EU member states, to transfer supervisory powers to the ECB, thanks to an article in the EU Treaty providing for this possibility. The ECB became as such the largest bank supervisor in the world, as measured by the total assets under its supervision. The decision to move in this direction was one of the three building blocks to restore confidence in the European financial system, together with the creation of the European Stability

Mechanism (ESM), and the outright monetary transactions (OMTs) of the ECB or the 'whatever it takes' assurances from its President Mario Draghi.

Recovery and Resolution, the Single Resolution Mechanism and the Deposit Guarantee Schemes (chapter 7). The element that proved the most challenging to harmonise – and probably also the most novel of the great plumbing exercise – was the requirement to put bank resolution schemes in place and the creation of resolution authorities. The non-existence of a specific resolution framework allowed banks to require state support, as they were too big, too complex or too interconnected to fail. The new framework, composed of mandatory bail-in and sector-sponsored resolution funds, together with pre-funded deposit protection schemes, should allow the authorities to manage a bank crisis in an orderly way, make failing banks resolvable and putting an end to the 'too-big-to-fail' dictum. In short, it should bring market discipline back into the banking sector.

The EU's State Aid Policy during the Crisis (chapter 8). The roughly 14% of GDP used during the crisis to bail out banks will be a drag on the EU member states' economies for some time to come. Not only is an important part of the financial system still state-owned, but the costs have also significantly increased state debts as a result of bail-outs. In accordance with EU Treaty rules, the EU imposed tight restructuring requirements on state-aided banks. But it has only been since the savings banks crisis in Spain that a significant form of burden-sharing with debt-holders was applied, which was spelled out in the EFSF (European Financial Stability Facility) Memorandum of Understanding on Financial Sector Policy Conditionality in Spain, dated July 2012. State aid policy will continue to form a cornerstone of the new resolution schemes, as the use of resolution funds will require authorisation under the EU's state aid rules.

Safe to bank? (chapter 9). Only the future will be able to tell us whether the new regulatory and supervisory framework works and whether it will be safe to bank. Considering the different layers and cushions that have been put in place (see Table 1), much will depend on the proper implementation and enforcement of the rules and the degree of toughness exercised by the supervisor. But policy-makers will also need to be vigilant in addressing the outstanding regulatory issues and give judicious consideration to new supervisory priorities.

Table 1. Financial re-regulation and supervision in a nutshell

Item	Before	New rules
Capital	Basel II/CRD	Basel III/CRD IV: More and better quality capital (up to more than the double)
OTC derivatives markets	No EU rules, bilateral trading	Central clearing (about 2/3 in CCPs, EMIR rules) and trading (MiFID II)
Rating agencies	No EU rules, 'freedom of speech'	License and supervision (CRA Regulation)
Hedge funds	No EU rules	License and supervision (AIFMD)
Resolution	No EU rules	Resolution authorities and funds, mandatory bail-in, single resolution authority (SRB) and fund
Deposit guarantee schemes	Minimum level of €20,000 (later increased to €100,000), no mandatory pre-funding	Pre-funding (0.8% deposits) and quick pay-out
Supervision	MoUs, Committees	European Supervisory Authorities (ESAs), Single Supervisory Mechanism (SSM), European Systemic Risk Board

References

Lannoo, Karel (2008), *Concrete Steps to More Integrated Oversight, The EU's Policy Response to the Financial Crisis,* CEPS Task Force Report, Centre for European Policy Studies, Brussels, December.

_____ (2014) "The G-20, five years on", CEPS Essay, CEPS, Brussels, March (www.ceps.eu/publications/g-20-five-years).

UK House of Commons (2008), "The run on the Rock", Fifth Report of Session 2007–08, Treasury Committee, 26 January, London.

Van Rompuy, H., J.M. Barroso, M. Draghi and J-C Juncker (2012), "Towards a Genuine Economic and Monetary Union" (Four Presidents Report), 26 June, Brussels.

2. CREDIT RATING AGENCIES: THE EARLY TARGETS*

Consensus on the need to regulate credit rating agencies (CRAs) emerged rapidly, even before Lehman Brothers filed for bankruptcy. As the first waves of the subprime crisis started to roll in, it rapidly became apparent that rating agencies bore a heavy responsibility for the lack of due diligence. This was even more the case in the EU, where, unlike the US, no regulation of rating agencies was in place until 2009.

The debate on the role of rating agents and the appropriate regulatory framework considerably pre-dates this crisis, however. As early as the 1997 Asian financial crisis, the delayed reaction of rating agents to the public finance situation of these countries was strongly criticised. The same criticism of CRAs was levelled when the dot.com bubble burst in 2001. Many reports were written on their role in that episode, but it was not until mid-2008 that a consensus emerged in the EU that the industry was in need of statutory legislation. In the meantime, the US had adopted the Credit Rating Agency Reform Act in 2006. At global level, in 2003, the International Organisation of Securities Commissions (IOSCO) adopted a Statement of Principles on the role of credit rating agencies – but apparently the initiative was not successful.

Rating agents pose a multitude of regulatory problems, none of which can be solved easily. Some of these are specific to the profession and the current market structure, whereas others are of a more generic nature. Some are related to basic principles of conduct in the financial services sector, while others are part of horizontal market regulation, such as market access and competition. The financial crisis also demonstrated the important

* This chapter extends and updates an earlier ECMI Policy Brief on the subject (see Lannoo, 2010). Valuable comments and input by Jan-Martin Frie are gratefully acknowledged.

role of rating agents in financial stability, which involves the new macro-prudential authorities.

This chapter starts with an overview of the credit rating industry today. The second section analyses the use of credit ratings and shows how the authorities created a captive or artificial market for CRAs. Section 3 briefly outlines the role of CRAs in the crisis, and section 4 reviews the EU CRA Regulation and its successive amendments. The chapter concludes with a comparison of proposals for regulatory reform of the sector, which remain, even after the new rules, unimplemented.

2.1 The credit rating industry today

The credit rating industry is a global business. Despite the fact that there are 27 registered and certified CRAs in the EU today, the rating industry worldwide as well as in the EU is controlled by a handful of players that are of US parentage. Standard & Poor's (S&P) and Moody's, taken together, accounted for a market share of 74.2% in the EU in 2013.[5] And with Fitch accounting for 16.2% that year, the 'Big 3' serviced an enormous 90.4% of the EU market. In certain market segments, such as ratings of structured finance products, the market share of the Big 3 is even higher, reaching 96% in the first half of 2014.[6] In 2012, 98.5% of their ratings were solicited i.e. the issuer of the product or the rated entity itself requested the rating.[7] A brief portrait of these three companies is given in Box 1.

Such an oligopolistic market structure can result in a sub-optimal degree of competition in the market. CRAs can afford to keep prices well above production costs, resulting in high mark-ups (and consequently unnecessarily high prices for clients and end-consumers). Figure 1 illustrates that the Big 3 achieved very high profit margins, ranging between 34-50% in 2013, which are just below the pre-crisis level for S&P and Moody's, and slightly higher for Fitch. Figure 1 also demonstrates that all three have recovered from the drop in revenues during the financial crisis, with S&P

---

[5] ESMA (2014b), Share of 2013 industry turnover generated from rating activities and ancillary services.

[6] ESMA (2014a, Table 1), based on a number of ratings outstanding.

[7] ESMA (2013, Table 6).

experiencing the slowest recovery and remaining just below its 2007 level in 2013.

Box 1. The 'Big Three' CRAs

Moody's was incorporated in 1914 as a bond-rating and investment analysis company. Today, the US-listed company Moody's Corporation is the parent company of Moody's Investors Service, which provides credit ratings and research on debt instruments and securities, and Moody's Analytics, which encompasses its non-ratings businesses, including risk-management software for financial institutions, quantitative credit analysis tools, economic research and other services. Combined, the group employs about 9,900 persons.

Standard & Poor's was incorporated in 1941, following the merger of two firms that were active in credit-risk analysis. Both firms originated from similar circumstances as Moody's, in the context of the huge industrial expansion of the US in the second half of the 19th and early 20th centuries. S&P was taken over by McGraw Hill in 1966, the US-listed media concern, and today forms the most important part of the group in terms of revenues, and even more so in profits (about 73%), although these seriously declined in the period 2007-11. S&P ratings services employ about 6,000 persons.

Fitch Ratings – by far the smaller originally 'European' player in the sector with headquarters in New York and London – is part of the Fitch Group, which also includes Fitch Solutions, a distribution channel for Fitch Ratings products, and Algorithmics, which provides risk-management services. The Fitch Group was a majority-owned subsidiary of the French Fimalac group, but the controlling stake was recently sold to the US media conglomerate Hearst. Fitch grew through acquisitions of several smaller rating agents, including IBCA and Duff & Phelps. Fitch Ratings employs around 2,000 persons.

Figure 1. Revenues and operating margins of the Big 3, 2007-13

Sources: ESMA supervision of Credit Rating Agencies and Trade Repositories - Annual report 2014 and work plan. 16 February 2015.

That the credit rating business is largely of American parentage should come as no surprise, as it is an intrinsic part of the market-driven system pioneered by the US. Unlike the bank-driven model found throughout Europe, a market-driven system relies on a multi-layered system to make it work (Black, 2001). Reputational intermediaries – such as investment banks, institutional investors, law firms and rating agents – and self-regulatory organisations – e.g. professional federations and standards-setters – play an important role in making the system, in between issuers and investors, work. In effect, financial markets are constantly affected by adverse selection mechanisms, and investors need third-party tools such as credit ratings in order to reduce asymmetric information and to improve their understanding of the riskiness of financial products.

Since there had not been much of a capital market in Europe until recently, banks have essentially performed the credit-risk analysis function, and continue to do so today. But the capacity of European banks to conduct credit-risk analysis declined, possibly as a result of the strong reputation of the US capital market model. The introduction of the euro and a set of EU regulatory measures led to the rapid development of European capital markets and a demand for ratings. Moreover, European authorities created a captive market for an essentially US-based industry.

2.2 A captive market for CRAs in the EU

Two forms of 'regulation' created a captive market for CRAs in the EU: Basel II, implemented in the EU as the capital requirements Directive, and the liquidity-providing operations of the European Central Bank. Both explicitly use the rating structure of CRAs to determine risk-weighting for capital requirement purposes, and 'haircuts' and minimum thresholds for the ECB's liquidity-providing operations.[8] The United States did not use either method to the same degree, as it did not implement Basel II (largely because the Federal Reserve did not want to have the vast majority of US banks relying on CRAs for setting regulatory risk weights), and the

---

[8] A haircut is a percentage deduction of the market value of securities held by banks.

discount window of the Fed is not based on ratings. The Dodd-Frank Wall Street Reform and Consumer Protection Act of July 2010 goes even further, requiring regulators to remove any references to "investment grade" and "credit ratings" of securities.[9]

This Basel II approach was not modified in Basel III, nor in the EU's CRD IV/CRR (capital requirements Regulation), which implements Basel III in European law (see chapter 5). In its 'standardised approach', to be used by less sophisticated banks, it bases risk weights on assessments by rating agents that qualify as an External Credit Assessment Institution (ECAI), discussed in more detail below. The capital requirements increase with the decline in the rating, from 0% for AA-rated (and higher) government bonds, or a minimum of 20% for banks and corporations, up to 150% for ratings of CCC or below (CRR Arts 116-125). But the risk weight is 0% for all sovereign debt in the European Economic Area (EEA) funded in domestic currency (CRR Art. 114). A zero-risk weight means that a bank does not have to set any capital aside for these assets. The new rules set criteria on how to use ECAIs' ratings (CRR Arts 138-141), and recommend banks to use other forms of credit assessment as well.

The use of rating agents is possibly even more prevalent in the assessment of marketable assets used as collateral in the ECB's liquidity-providing operations. The credit assessment for eligible collateral is predominantly based on a public rating, issued by an eligible ECAI. In the ECB's definition, an ECAI is an institution whose credit assessments may be used by credit institutions for determining the risk weight of exposures according to the CRD.[10] The minimum credit-quality threshold is defined in terms of a 'single A' credit assessment, which was temporarily relaxed during the financial crisis to BBB-.[11] If multiple and possibly conflicting ECAI assessments exist for the same issuer/debtor or guarantor, the

---

[9] Public Law 111 - 203 - Dodd-Frank Wall Street Reform and Consumer Protection Act (www.gpo.gov/fdsys/pkg/PLAW-111publ203/pdf/PLAW-111publ203.pdf).

[10] See ECB (2006, p. 43).

[11] "Single A" means a minimum long-term rating of "A-" by Fitch or Standard & Poor's, or an "A" rating by Moody's (see ECB, 2006, p. 41).

first-best rule (i.e. the best available ECAI credit assessment) is applied.[12]

The liquidity categories for marketable assets are subdivided into five categories, based on issuer classification and asset type, with an increasing level of valuation haircuts, depending on the residual maturity.[13] An important group of assets in the context of the financial crisis, classified as 'category V', are the asset-backed securities (ABS), or securitisation instruments. The extent to which banks used ABS collateral in liquidity operations rose dramatically after mid-2007, from 4% in 2004 to 18% in 2007 and 28% in 2008 (Fitch, 2010, p. 7). Within ABS, residential mortgage-backed securities (RMBS) form the most important element, exceeding 50%. These securitisation instruments, and in particular the residential mortgage-backed securities segment, were an extremely important market for CRAs. Moody's, for example, assigned the AAA rating to 42,625 RMBS from 2000 to 2007 (9,029 mortgage-backed securities in 2006 alone) "like in a factory", but later had to downgrade the assets.[14]

2.3 Credit ratings and the crisis

In 2007, 89% of those originally rated as investment grade were reduced to junk status. Critics claim that the poor performance of credit ratings in the structured finance segment was due to the particular market concentration in this segment, reducing the need to compete over the quality of ratings and increasing the incentive to issue complacent ratings instead. Until the financial crisis hit, the Big 3 dominated the market, obtaining a share of close to 100% (ESMA, 2014a, p. 9). Conflicts of interest become even more apparent when market concentration is also present on the supply

---

[12] See ECB (2008, p. 42).

[13] The liquidity categories were changed in September 2008 and the valuation haircuts increased in July 2010. See changes to risk-control measures in Eurosystem credit operations, European Central Bank, Press Notices, 4 September 2008 and 28 July 2010.

[14] As characterised by Phil Angelides, Chairman of the 10-member Financial Crisis Inquiry Commission appointed by the US government to investigate the causes of the financial crisis, and quoted in Bloomberg, 2 June 2010.

side, i.e. the issuer side. In 2007, the top 12 underwriters of mortgage-backed securities (MBS) controlled over 80% of the market.[15] This would be less of a problem if the investor were to pay for the rating, but under the issuer-pays model, this raises particular concerns as the underwriters of MBS could probably exert considerable pressure on the CRAs. In 2006, the share of structured finance ratings of the overall revenue was on average 50% or more (CESR, 2008, p. 8), which emphasises the reliance of the CRAs on this market segment. Lawsuits related to inflated and improper ratings on structured finance products forced Standard & Poor's in 2015 to pay a record $1.37 billion in a settlement with state and federal prosecutors in the US.[16] Similarly, Moody's is currently under investigation by the US Department of Justice.

The reference to credit ratings in regulation and risk models resulted in a 'cliff effect' and put CRAs under the spotlight as the crisis unfolded. A cliff effect is created when the rating of an entity or a security has dropped below a certain threshold, rendering it ineligible for certain regulatory purposes such as the ECB operations.[17] In this case, the securities of the entity are sold and a fire sale begins, where multiple actors try to sell the same product amidst sharply declining liquidity and prices. A downward spiral is set in motion and the market price no longer adequately reflects the value of the security. As the issuer comes under pressure, the rating drops further and also affects the rating of entities holding the security.

In the case of sovereigns, this cliff effect is particularly strong and directly affects the respective banking sector, which is usually highly exposed to the sovereign through bond holdings and implicit guarantees. The downgrade of a sovereign also has direct effects on the ratings of many non-sovereign issuers, since CRAs usually do not issue ratings more than a few notches above the rating of the sovereign in which the issuer resides. The Financial Stability Board,

[15] As reported by Professor John Coffee in OECD (2010), Hearings on Competition and Credit Rating Agencies, 5 October, p. 9.

[16] US Department of Justice, 3 February 2015.

[17] The European Commission (2011, footnote 29) defines cliff effects as "sudden actions that are triggered by a rating downgrade under a specific threshold, where downgrading a single security can have a disproportionate cascading effect".

under the G-20 umbrella, strongly recommended a change in market practices, providing principles to mitigate excessive reliance on ratings and to limit the risk of cliff effects that could result from legal and market practices. These measures are equally intended to improve the quality of credit ratings as such as they encourage investors to perform their own in-house credit analysis.

2.4 The EU rating agencies regulation and its successive amendments

As the subprime crisis started to unfold, a policy consensus rapidly emerged that rating agents should be regulated at EU level. The proposal for a regulation was published in November 2008 and adopted in April 2009, which was a minimum interval in EU decision-making.[18] The regulation was the first new EU legislative measure triggered by the financial crisis. It was also one of the first financial services measures to be issued as a regulation, meaning it is directly applicable, unlike a directive, which has to be implemented in national law.

The EU was not starting from scratch, however. Back in 2004, further to an own initiative report of the European Parliament (Katifioris report), the European Commission asked the Committee of European Securities Regulators (CESR) for technical advice regarding market practice and competitive problems in the CRAs. In a Communication (European Commission, 2006) published in December 2005, it decided that no legislation was needed for three reasons: 1) three EU directives already covered rating agents indirectly: the 2003 market abuse Directive (MAD), the CRD and MiFID (markets in financial instruments Directive); 2) a code of conduct for credit rating agencies was published by the International Organisation of Securities Commissions (IOSCO) in 2004;[19] and 3) self-regulation by the sector, following the IOSCO code.[20]

---

[18] Regulation (EC) 1060/2009 of the European Parliament and of the Council of 16 September 2009 on credit rating agencies.

[19] See www.iosco.org/library/pubdocs/pdf/IOSCOPD180.pdf

[20] Communication from the Commission on Credit Rating Agencies (2006/C 59/02), OJ C 59/2 of 11.03.2006. It should be added that rating agents were

In 2006, in a report for the Commission, CESR concluded that the rating agents largely complied with the IOSCO code.[21] But concerns remained regarding the oligopoly in the sector, the treatment of confidential information, the role of ancillary services and unsolicited ratings. In a follow-up report published in May 2008, focusing especially on structured finance, CESR strongly recommended following the international market-driven approach by improving the IOSCO code. Tighter regulation would not have prevented the problems emerging from the loans to the US subprime housing market, according to CESR.

Notwithstanding the CESR's advice, the Commission went ahead and issued a proposal in November 2008, after two consultations in July and September 2008. It was virtually agreed by the European Parliament in a single reading by April 2009, and formally adopted in September 2009.

The Regulation came into force 20 days after its publication in the Official Journal, on 7 December 2009. But guidance had to be provided by CESR before the Regulation could take effect, by 7 June 2010, regarding registration, supervision, the endorsement regime and supervisory reporting; and by 7 September 2010, regarding enforcement practices, rating methodologies and certification. CESR, later reconfigured as ESMA, has to report annually on the application.

The Regulation (CRA I) provided for EU-wide definitions, standards on organisational requirements, supervision, transparency and conflict of interest as well as for a third-country equivalence regime. Two amendments were made to this initial Regulation shortly after it entered into force. The first amendment (CRA II)[22] tabled by the Commission on 2 June 2010, and adopted on 21 March 2011, modified the Regulation to centralise the regulation, registration and day-to-day supervision of CRAs at

---

exempted from the market abuse directive (2003/125/EC) rules on conflicts of interest disclosure (see Di Noia & Micossi, 2010, p. 65).

[21] CESR's Report to the European Commission on the compliance of Credit Rating Agencies with the IOSCO code, CESR (2006), 06-545.

[22] Regulation (EU) No 513/2011 of the European Parliament and of the Council of 11 May 2011 amending Regulation (EC) No 1060/2009 on credit rating agencies.

European level with ESMA, as originally envisaged by the high-level de Larosière (2009) report. National supervisors remain responsible for the supervision of the use of credit ratings by financial institutions, and can request ESMA to withdraw a license. The amendment also introduced definitions of infringements and sanctions and gave ESMA the power to impose fines for failure to respect provisions of the regulations (see Art. 36 and Annex II). ESMA may also delegate specific supervisory tasks to national authorities. The amendment, however, does not propose any specific involvement of the European Systemic Risk Board (ESRB) \, which could have been useful in the control of the methodologies and the macroeconomic models used by CRAs.

A second amendment (CRA III)[23] was proposed by the European Commission on 15 November 2011, in the midst of the euro sovereign crisis, to curtail the market power of rating agents. CRA III, which was formally adopted in May 2013, made some significant changes and introduced new provisions. The changes chiefly relate to conflict of interest stemming from the issuer-pays model, competition in the market, overreliance on external ratings and special provisions governing the rating of sovereigns. CRA III also extended the scope of the Regulation to rating outlooks and credit watches, which can be interpreted as important components of a credit rating. The key provisions of the Regulation relate to transparency, conflicts of interest, competition, overreliance and third-country access.

2.4.1 *Transparency*

Transparency requirements impact the market for ratings in a number of ways. Increased transparency leads to more competition as it facilitates unsolicited ratings, reduces conflicts of interest and increases market stability as disclosure of information allows for internal risk modelling, thereby decreasing reliance on credit ratings.

---

[23] Regulation (EU) No 462/2013 of the European Parliament and of the Council of 21 May 2013 amending Regulation (EC) No 1060/2009 on credit rating agencies and Directive 2013/14/EU of the European Parliament and of the Council of 21 May 2013 amending Directive 2003/41/EC, Directive 2009/65/EC and Directive 2011/61/EU.

The Regulation requires CRAs to disclose their methodologies, models and rating assumptions. ESMA is mandated to set standards for methodologies and also introduced CEREP, as a central repository where CRAs are mandated to publish historical performance data and information about their methodologies. One important aspect in terms of transparency to the markets is the annual transparency report (description of internal control mechanisms, allocation of staff, record-keeping policy, revenue information etc.). Periodic disclosure obligations on rating agencies include, among others, the requirement to disclose their 20 largest clients in terms of revenue.

CRA II added additional transparency requirements for the structured finance segment. Especially in the area of structured product ratings, the CRAs had failed to adequately assess risks in the underlying assets in the run-up to the crisis. CRA II requires issuers, originators and sponsors of structured finance instruments to jointly disclose the same information about credit quality and performance of the underlying assets that they have given to the CRA, as is the case in the US under the SEC's Rule 17g-5. This change was welcomed by the markets as it would make both regimes comparable and restore confidence in the securitisation market. Disclosure of this information should also enable the publication of unsolicited ratings and spur competition in this market segment. In 2012, for example, all ratings on structured finance products were issued on a solicited basis (ESMA, 2013a). The extent to which this disclosure process will work is questionable as ratings on structured finance products are complex and require substantial resources.

Another novelty with respect to transparency in the market is the European Rating Platform (Article 11a), to be administered by ESMA. Starting from 1 January 2016, all ratings issued on a solicited, i.e. an issuer-pays basis, must be reported to ESMA, which will publish this on the European Rating Platform.[24] This measure aims at increasing oversight and comparability between ratings.

---

[24] This is not applicable to the investor-pays model, as it would erode its profitability. On 30 September 2014, the Commission published the applicable technical standards in a delegated Regulation (see OJ, L 2/24 of 6.01.2015).

Finally, CRA III introduced some requirements with respect to sovereign ratings. CRAs are required to regularly publish a calendar with a timeline for the publication of sovereign ratings for the coming 12 months. Ratings should be published only after close of business of trading venues, in order to allow market participants to incorporate the rating event into their decision-making process. Sovereign ratings should be reviewed every six months and not include policy recommendations.

2.4.2 Conflicts of interest

A proper identification, disclosure and management of conflicts of interest are crucial to preserve market trust and integrity. Transparency measures can be seen as equally effective in preventing conflicts of interest as the requirement to disclose potential conflicts of interest and the names of the rated entities providing more than 5% of the rating company's annual revenues. Furthermore, CRA I sets operational requirements to ensure the independence of employees of CRAs, such as a mandatory rotation of analysts and the prohibition of an analyst's involvement in negotiations of fees. Analysts' remuneration should also not depend on the revenues generated from the entities they rate.

CRA III addresses conflicts of interest that could arise where the same investors hold considerable capital or voting rights in more than one CRA. The threshold in terms of capital and voting rights in one CRA is set at 5%, which prohibits an investor to hold 5% or more in another CRA.[25] It further stipulates that a CRA shall abstain from issuing a rating, where a shareholder or member holding 10% of the voting rights of that agency: i) is also holding 10% or more of the rated entity, ii) is a member of the administrative or supervisory board of that rated entity or iii) where the rated entity holds 10% or more of the CRA. CRA I had only addressed this type of conflict of interest with respect to analysts' ratings.

The latest amendment introduces a general civil liability regime in the absence of a contractual relationship between the investor and the CRA in the case of issuer-pays models. Civil

---

[25] The 5% threshold corresponds to the threshold set in the Transparency Directive (Directive 2004/109/EC), above which an entity needs to disclose the shareholding.

liability relates to infringements that had an impact on the rating outcome and were done "intentionally or [with] gross negligence". Although it will be difficult to prove that an infringement was done intentionally or with gross negligence, this measure sends the right signal and acts as a strong incentive for CRAs not to issue complacency ratings. A further amendment established that fees should not be discriminatory and are justifiable only where actual costs differ and that fees should be disclosed to ESMA. This measure should allow ESMA to detect market abuse.

Given the complexity of structured finance products and their role in the crisis, special provisions to avoid conflict of interest in relation in this market segment have been part of the regulatory framework from the initial regulation. CRA I encouraged CRAs to inform clients about the specificities of structure finance ratings compared to ratings on traditional investments and required that structured finance ratings should be clearly identifiable as such (Article 10(3) CRAI). CRA III introduced a rotation mechanism, for the CRA (Article 6b), by defining a maximum 4-year duration of any contractual relationship between issuers and CRAs and a minimum period during which the CRA is prohibited from entering into a new contract.[26] The provision only applies to the issuer-pays model and is targeted at related conflicts of interest. For the time being, the rotation mechanism is limited to re-securitisation products with underlying assets from the same originator in order to allow for gradual adjustment in the market.[27] The Commission will have to report to the Council and the Parliament by 1 January 2016 on the appropriateness of extending the rotation to other products, whether a different maximum duration of the contractual relationship is warranted and whether a hand-over file should be produced by the outgoing CRA to limit the loss of information when the new CRA comes in.

---

[26] Where this period is equal to the duration of the expired contract.

[27] A re-securitisation product is a financial instrument where (at least one of) the underlying assets is a securitisation product. The rotation mechanism has been introduced to re-securitisation only, as the default risk of a re-securitised product depends much less on the debt servicing capacity of the issuer itself, as for instance in the case of a corporate bond. Hence the loss of information from limiting long-lasting relationship is relatively low (CRA III, Recital 14).

2.4.3 Competition

Many of the measures on transparency and conflict of interest are also meant to stimulate competition, such as the rotation requirement. Transparency measures are also intended to increase competition in the market as they allow users of ratings to better understand and compare the quality of ratings as well as reduce barriers to entry.

One instrument is aimed at supporting small- and medium-sized CRAs (SME CRAs) in the market, with exemptions for the provisions on independence and avoidance of conflicts of interest (Art. 6), for the requirement to establish a review function and for the rotation requirement introduced by CRA III, with the latter exemption again specifically aimed at fostering competition in the highly concentrated structured finance segment. CRA III introduced the requirement to appoint an SME CRA (Art. 8d)[28] where multiple credit ratings have been solicited, and requires an issuer to solicit at least two CRAs where a rating of a structured finance instrument is solicited (Art. 8c). The obligation to appoint an SME CRA, however, is merely based on a comply-or-explain enforcement mechanism, calling into question its effectiveness.

A provision in CRA III also foresaw the creation of a network of SME CRAs in which they bundle resources and have a bigger impact on the market. But after consulting the market participants, the Commission's feasibility report May 2014 concluded that such a network has no support among stakeholders at this point and has not been pursued further since (European Commission, 2014).

2.4.4 Overreliance – captive market

As a response to the financial crisis, several initiatives were launched to reduce reliance on credit ratings, by market participants as well as by regulators, and to implement alternatives to credit ratings (FSB, 2010 and 2012). The CRA III is the European equivalent of these efforts at international level. The amendment for the first time mentions that credit ratings have a regulatory value and aims

---

[28] Where a small- and medium-sized CRA is defined as a CRA with a share of no more than 10% of the EU market. Market share here is measured with reference to the annual turnover generated from credit-rating activities and ancillary services, at group level (CRA III, Art. 8d(3)).

at reducing the captive market for CRAs. To this end, the amendment stipulates that central banks should perform their own credit assessments as outlined in FSB principles and encourages financial institutions not to rely solely on credit ratings.

On the side of the regulators and supervisors, the ESAs (EBA, EIOPA and ESMA) and the ESRB are obliged to refrain from referring to ratings in their guidelines, recommendations and technical standards where this would trigger cliff effects. The ESAs have been working to identify and where possible to remove, by 31 December 2015, all references to ratings in their guidelines and recommendations and to mitigate the over-reliance on ratings (EBA, EIOPA & ESMA, 2014a and 2014b). By the end of 2015, the Commission has to report to the Council and the European Parliament on the steps taken thus far to delete references and to identify alternatives to external credit ratings. Based on this report, the Commission will have to assess whether all references to credit ratings in EU law can be deleted by 2020. This ambitious exercise is laudable, but probably illusory, given the continued reliance on ratings in the capital regulation of banks (CRD IV).

2.4.5   Third-country equivalence

Since the industry is essentially of US parentage, a focal point in the discussions has been the third-country regime. The Regulation states that CRAs established in a third country may apply for certification, provided that they are registered and subject to supervision in their home country, and that the Commission has adopted an equivalence decision. However, credit ratings issued in a third country can only be used if they are not of systemic importance to the EU's financial stability (CRA I, Art. 5.1), meaning that all large CRAs need to be fully registered in the EU. In addition, credit ratings produced outside the EU have to be endorsed by the CRA registered in the EU, subject to a series of conditions (Art. 4.3). So far the legal and supervisory framework of the US, Canada, Australia, Japan, Argentina, Brazil, Hong Kong, Mexico and Singapore have been recognised as equivalent to the requirements set out by the CRA Regulation.

Box 2. The Dodd-Frank Bill and CRAs

The EU regime for CRAs is comparable to the US regime, as introduced by the Dodd-Frank Bill. Whereas the US had already regulated the sector in 2006 with the Credit Rating Agency Reform Act, this was a light regime requiring CRAs to register with the Securities and Exchange Commission (SEC) in Washington, D.C., as a Nationally Recognized Statistical Rating Organization (NRSRO). The Dodd-Frank Bill fundamentally alters this regime by requiring tight operational (internal controls, conflicts of interest, qualification standards for credit rating analysts) and governance requirements, and detailed disclosure requirements (including disclosure of the methodologies used). The SEC implemented the measures of the Bill on 18 May 2011, and created an Office of Credit Ratings to issue penalties and to conduct annual examinations and reports.

Sources: SEC website, Cinquegrana (2009) and Clifford Chance (2010).

2.5 The regulatory debate

The EU's regulations do not fundamentally alter the problem that CRAs pose from a public policy perspective: 1) the oligopolistic nature of the industry, 2) the potential conflict of interest through the issuer-pays principle and 3) the public good of private ratings. The EU approach seems to be a second-best solution. A more fundamental review is needed of the business model of the CRAs, and which other industry sectors could provide a useful alternative model.

The oligopolistic nature of the industry was addressed in the Regulation in several ways, such as the conflict-of-interest provisions arising from the issuer-pays model. Despite these rules and an increasing number of registered and certified CRAs, the market remains highly concentrated. Nevertheless, the effects of some of the provisions of the latest amendments still need to be assessed and will take time to fully materialise. The report by the Commission and ESMA to the Council and the Parliament at the end of 2015 should be revealing in this regard.

Measures to wean asset management companies from their reliance on external credit ratings and the deletion of references to external credit ratings in legislation can be expected to reduce the captive market for credit ratings. And they should also have a positive impact on competition. But whether increased competition will eventually improve the quality of ratings is questionable, as research finds that more competition would not necessarily improve standards. New entrants do not necessarily improve the quality of ratings – on the contrary. They attract business by friendly and inflated ratings. As competition reduces future rents, it increases the risk of the short-term gains by cheating.

In an analysis of the corporate bond markets, Becker & Milbourn (2009) found a significant positive correlation between the degree of competition and the level of the credit ratings. Concretely, they noticed a positive correlation between Fitch's entry into the market and ratings levels, without exception. These findings are not surprising given the predominance of the issuer-pays model and the inability of the dataset used to distinguish between solicited and unsolicited ratings. Due to the issuer-pays model, the CRAs compete for the supply side of the industry (i.e. the issuer) not the demand side (i.e. the investor). The CRA Regulation does not change this situation.

On the structure of the industry, it could be argued that the EU is actually increasing the barriers to entry by introducing a license and setting tight regulation, rather than taking the oligopolistic nature as one of the fundamental reasons for the abuses. In addition, since statutory supervision of the industry may increase moral hazard, it gives a regulatory 'blessing' and may further reduce the incentives for banks to conduct proper risk assessments.

In their contribution to a VoxEU report, Pagano & Volpin (2009) propose an even more drastic solution in which ratings would be paid for by the investors. The investor-pays model was dominant in the US until the 1970s, but because of increasingly complex securities in need of large resources and the fear of declining revenues resulting from the dissemination of private ratings through new information technologies, the issuer-pays principle was introduced. Pagano & Volpin do not discuss how to deal with free riding, but moving back to the investor-pays principle may also require further regulation to prohibit the sale of ancillary services by CRAs to issuers. The EU Regulation goes in the direction of requiring more disclosure (see Annex I, Section E of the Regulation), but it is questionable whether investors will read this.

On the contrary, given that a supervisory fiat has been given, investors may be even less inclined to read all the information, as was demonstrated during the financial crisis.

Ponce (2009) discusses an interesting alternative to the issuer-pays and investor-pays models: the platform-pays model. He demonstrates on the basis of large data sets that the transition from the investor-pays to the issuer-pays model had a negative impact on the quality of the ratings. Under the issuer-pays model, a rating agency may choose a quality standard below the socially efficient level. In this case, Ponce argues, a rating agency does not internalise the losses that investors bear from investing in low-quality securities. A rating agent may give ratings to low-quality securities in order to increase its revenues. To avoid this, Ponce proposes the 'platform-pays' model, which takes the form of a clearing house for ratings, complemented by prudential oversight of ratings' quality to control for bribery. The platform assigns the agent (based on performance and experience), and the issuer pays up front. This would at the same time overcome the oligopoly problem. The problem with this model, however, is that its governance will need to be watertight. An alternative to this model is the Rating Fund, whereby both issuers and investors would contribute to a fund, which would assign ratings based on performance (Kotecha et al., 2010).

A variant of this latter idea is the creation of a privately funded but European rating agency, proposed by the German management guru Roland Berger (2012). Berger sees many weaknesses in the current structure of the rating industry – namely being too US-centred, oligopolistic and ridden with conflicts of interest – and proposes to find a European investor base to fund a European agency. Investors would, in his proposal, also pay for ratings, but a central credit platform should consolidate all credit data outside the banking system, covering the ratings as well as data about issuers. The contractual relationship, however, would remain between issuers and rating agencies.

At the other end of these proposals stands the idea of creating a publicly funded European rating agency. CRA III mandated a full exploration of two questions: i) the appropriateness of developing a creditworthiness assessment of sovereign debt and ii) the feasibility and desirability of setting up a European credit rating foundation for all other credit ratings (Art. 39b). The Commission was tasked with reporting to the Council and the Parliament on these two questions by 31 December 2014 and 31 December 2016 (Recital 43), respectively. This idea was broadly discussed in the midst of the sovereign debt crisis, when a succession of downgrades of sovereigns followed one another at an increasing pace, whereas CRAs had not seen the problem coming. The initial downgrade for Greece, for example, only happened in early 2009 when the country was about to receive a first serious warning from the EU Council (starting from the A or A+ level to CCC or sovereign default in 2012), or even later for Portugal and Ireland (see Lannoo et al., 2011).

Given that incentives and reputation are key to the functioning of the ratings business, Larry Harris (2010) proposes an entirely different approach. Taking inspiration from the debate over bonuses in the banking sector, he proposes to defer part of the bonuses based on results. Given that credit ratings are about the future, the performance of the securities rated would be the indicator of the fee CRAs can charge. An important part of the fees would be put into a fund, against which the rating agencies could borrow to finance their operations. Disclosure of these deferred contingent compensation schemes would be required, so that investors can decide for themselves which schemes provide adequate incentives.

Another possibility for creating the right incentives is to move to a partnership structure in the CRA business, as is common in the audit sector, which share several characteristics in common with rating agencies. These include notably the type of work, the importance of reputation and global presence, the network economies and the oligopolistic structure, and the conflicts of interest. The audit sector is regulated by EU Directive (2006/43/EC, amended by 2014/56/EU), which brought the sector under statutory supervision. It sets tight rules on the governance and independence of auditing firms, and on quality control, and limits the provision of non-auditing services to an audit client. The downside of the partnership model, however, is the liability problem, which will deter many firms from being active in that way, although the second amendment to the CRA Regulation introduces a form of civil liability for rating agencies as well.

2.6 Assessment and conclusions

Considering the policy alternatives outlined above, the EU and the US should probably have considered the specificities of the sector more carefully before embarking on legislation. The legislation that was adopted does not alter the business model of the industry and gives rise to side effects, the most important of which is the supervisory seal, or the licence to issue ratings. Given the depth of the financial crisis and the central role played by rating agents, a more profound change would have been useful, towards the 'platform-pays' model or a long-term incentive structure, as discussed above. In the meantime and given the continued dominance of the issuer-pays model, the second-best solution is to increase transparency and mitigate conflicts of interest.

Under the new structure, ESMA is given a central role in the supervision of CRAs, but the question remains whether it can cope. The supervisor needs to check compliance with the basic requirements to decide on a licence and to verify adherence to the governance, operational, methodological and disclosure requirements imposed on CRAs. This is a heavy workload, especially considering that no supervision had been in place until 2010. First indications, however, promising, with ESMA creating a data base to compare ratings performance, and having registered, by the end of 2014, 27 different rating agents. In-depth investigations by ESMA into structured finance ratings (ESMA, 2014a) and into sovereign ratings (ESMA, 2013b) were important exercises that should be conducted on a regular basis. These inquiries also target other asset classes and include smaller CRAs.

The CRA market remains highly concentrated, even if the market share of the top 3 firms seems to be declining to about 90% today, from over 94% before the crisis.[29] Given the issuer-pays model and the inherent conflict of interest as revealed during the crisis, it is important to make sure that ESMA has sufficient resources to effectively monitor the CRAs. The recent budget cuts of the ESAs are not encouraging in this regard.

---

[29] In the segment for structured finance, the Canada-based CRA DBRS has managed to enter the market and captured 4% by the first half of 2014 (ESMA, 2014a, Table 1). In 2013, two more CRAs entered the market, but their market share remains marginal.

ESMA should make full use of its powers to closely supervise this vital sector. Where a situation arises in which penalties are appropriate, it could be considered to prohibit a credit rating agency from issuing ratings for a given period or in a given segment, as was done in the United States. The SEC denied the US-based CRA Egan-Jones the regulatory seal for certain ratings over a period of 18 months in 2013. Such a measure threatens the revenue streams of CRAs, helps to restore market integrity and equally gives a boost to smaller competitors.

More generally, the advantage of having a regulatory framework in place is that the Commission's competition directorate can start scrutinising the sector from its perspective. To our knowledge, the competition-policy dimensions of the CRA industry in Europe have not been closely investigated, as no commonly agreed definitions or tools were available at EU level and since the sector is essentially of US parentage. EU registration for the large CRAs will allow the authorities to verify their compliance with EU Treaty rules on concerted practices and abuse of dominant position, which may raise some feathers.

References

Arbak, Emrah and Piero Cinquegrana (2008), Report of the CEPS-ECMI Joint Workshop on the Reform of Credit Rating Agencies, November (www.eurocapitalmarkets.org).

Becker, Bo and Todd Milbourn (2009), *Reputation and competition: Evidence from the credit rating industry*, Harvard Business School, Working Paper No. 09-051, Cambridge, MA.

Black, Bernard S. (2001), "The legal and institutional preconditions for strong securities markets", *UCLA Law Review*, Vol. 48, pp. 781-855.

CESR (2008), "The role of credit rating agencies in structured finance", Consultation Paper, Committee of European Securities Regulators, Paris, February.

Cinquegrana, Piero (2009), "The Reform of the Credit Rating Agencies: A Comparative Perspective", ECMI Policy Brief, European Capital Markets Institute, Brussels, February (www.ceps.eu and www.eurocapitalmarkets.org).

Clifford Chance (2010), "Dodd-Frank Wall Street Reform and Consumer Protection Act", Client Briefing Report, July.

Coffee, John (2010), "Ratings Reform: A Policy Primer on Proposed, Pending and Possible Credit Rating Reforms", paper presented at a meeting of the OECD Competition Committee, 16 June, Paris.

de Larosière, Jacques (2009), Report of the High-Level Group on Financial Supervision in the EU, 25 February, Brussels.

Di Noia, Carmina, Stefano Micossi, Jacopo Carmassi and Fabrizia Peirce (2010), *Keep it Simple, Policy Response to the Financial Crisis*, CEPS Paperback, Centre for European Policy Studies, Brussels.

EBA, EIOPA and ESMA (2014a), "*Final Report on Mechanistic references to credit ratings in the ESAs' guidelines and recommendations*", February.

_____ (2014b), "The Use of Credit Ratings by Financial Intermediaries - Article 5(a) of the CRA Regulation", Discussion Paper, February.

ECB (2006), "The Implementation of Monetary Policy in the Euro Area", General documentation on Eurosystem monetary policy instruments and procedures, European Central Bank, Frankfurt, September.

_____ (2008), "The Implementation of Monetary Policy in the Euro Area", General documentation on Eurosystem monetary policy instruments and procedures, European Central Bank, Frankfurt, November.

ESMA (2013a), Technical Advice on the feasibility of a network of small and medium-sized CRAs, European Securities and Markets Authority, Paris, November.

_____ (2013b), Credit Rating Agencies, ESMA's assessment of governance, conflict of interest, resourcing adequacy and confidentiality controls, European Securities and Markets Authority, Paris, 2 December.

_____ (2014a), Credit Rating Agencies, ESMA's investigation into structured finance ratings, European Securities and Markets Authority, Paris, 16 December.

_____ (2014b), Credit Rating Agencies' 2014 market share calculations for the purposes of Article 8d of the CRA Regulation, European Securities and Markets Authority, Paris, 22 December.

_____ (2014c), 2015 Work Programme, European Securities and Markets Authority, Paris, 30 September.

_____ (2015), ESMA supervision of Credit Rating Agencies and Trade Repositories - Annual report 2014 and work plan, European Securities and Markets Authority, Paris, 16 February.

European Commission (2005), Communication from the Commission on Credit Rating Agencies, (2006/C 59/02), published in the Official Journal, 11 March 2006.

_____ (2008), Commission staff working document accompanying the proposal for a regulation of the European Parliament and of the Council on Credit Rating Agencies – Impact assessment, SEC/2008/2746 final, November.

_____ (2011), Commission staff working paper impact assessment accompanying the Proposal for a Regulation amending Regulation (EC) No 1060/2009 on credit rating agencies, 15 November.

_____ (2014), Report from the Commission to the Council and the European Parliament on the feasibility of a network of smaller credit rating agencies, May.

FSB (2010) "Principles for Reducing Reliance on CRA Ratings", Financial Stability Board, Basel, October.

_____ (2012), "Roadmap and workshop for reducing reliance on CRA ratings", Financial Stability Board, Basel, November.

Fitch Ratings (2010), "The Role of the ECB –Temporary Prop or Structural Underpinning?", Special Report, 11 May.

Harris, Larry (2010), "Pay the rating agencies according to results", *Financial Times*, 4 June.

IMF (2010), Global Financial Stability Report, International Monetary Fund, Washington, D.C., September

Kotecha, Mahesh, Sharon Ryan and Roy Weinberger (2010), "The Future of Structured Finance Ratings after the Financial Crisis", *Journal of Structured Finance*, Winter.

Lannoo, Karel (2010), "What reforms for the credit rating industry? A European perspective", ECMI Policy Brief No. 17, European Capital Markets Institute, Brussels, October.

Lannoo, Karel, Gunther Tichy, Owain ap Gwilym, Donato Masciandaro, Bartholomew Paudyn and Rasha Alsakka (2011), "Credit Rating Agencies: Part of the Solution or Part of the Problem?", *Intereconomics*, Forum, Vol. 46, No. 5, September-October, pp. 232-262.

OECD (2010), Hearings on Competition and Credit Rating Agencies, Competition Committee, Organisation for Economic Cooperation and Development, Paris, October.

Pagano, Marco and Paolo Volpin (2009), "Credit Ratings Failures: Causes and Policy Options", in Mathias Dewatripont, Xavier Freixas and Richard Portes (eds), *Macroeconomic Stability and Financial Regulation: Key Issues for the G20*, VoxEU, 2 March (www.voxeu.org/index.php?q=node/3167).

Ponce, Jorge (2009), "The Quality of Credit Ratings: A Two-Sided Market Perspective", August (www.bcu.gub.uy/autoriza/peiees/jor/2009/iees03j3471009.pdf).

Richardson, Matthew and Lawrence J. White (2009), "The Rating Agencies: Is regulation the answer?", in Viral V. Acharya and Matthew Richardson (eds), *Restoring Financial Stability*, New York, NY: Wiley.

Roland Berger (2012), The European Rating Agency Project, May.

US Department of Justice (2015), "Justice Department and State Partners Secure $1.375 Billion Settlement with S&P for Defrauding Investors in the Lead Up to the Financial Crisis", Press Release, 3 February.

3. GAME CHANGE IN ASSET MANAGEMENT*

The regulatory context for the European asset management industry changed more drastically than was initially expected at the beginning of the crisis. Despite claims by the industry that they were not responsible for the crisis, policy makers clearly thought differently. New rules concern hedge funds and private equity, on which no European framework had previously existed, restrictions on remuneration, tighter rules for depositaries, a more aligned supervisory framework plus all that is expected still to emerge out of the 'shadow banking' hat. But great opportunities are opening up to the asset management industry as Europe seeks to reduce the reliance on bank funding and the pension gap.

In regulatory terms, the wider asset management industry as such does not exist. Rather, the applicable rules depend on the particular license that the financial institution in question possesses. One may be licensed as a fund management company, a bank, an insurance undertaking, a pension fund or a broker. Broker. (Table 2 presents an overview of the applicable regulatory regimes). These various classifications immediately raise the question of possible inconsistencies, duplication or arbitrage among regimes. For certain segments of the asset management business, there is no question of which regulatory regime governs their operations, as they unambiguously fall into one of the aforementioned categories; for others, however, the vertical regulatory framework does not lend itself well to the range of activities they undertake.

---

* An earlier version of this chapter appeared in Karel Lannoo and Mirzha de Manuel Aramendía, "Game Change in Asset Management", in Michael Pinedo and Ingo Walter (eds), *Global Asset Management*, SimCorp StrategyLab, 2013. Valuable research assistance from Cosmina Amariei is gratefully acknowledged.

The crisis, however, has not lead to more convergence across regimes, on the contrary. The vertical segmentation of the industry, because of systemic and prudential reasons, seemed to be appropriate in the view of policy makers.

This segmentation of the financial industry implies that the diversity across the EU of the institutional framework will continue to be with us for some time to come. The crisis has strengthened financial disintegration, reducing the pressure for regulatory convergence, although asset-allocation patterns may have become more aligned across countries. The differences in consumer preferences, cultural habits and institutional heritage will thus remain a fundamental part of the European financial-markets landscape for some time to come.

The alternative investment fund managers Directive (AIFMD) should bring more EU-wide convergence to the regulation of the typical activities of asset managers: discretionary management, mandates and alternative investment funds. Hence UCITS (Undertakings for Collective Investments in Transferable Securities) remains the traditional investment fund regime, while a new pillar has been added for alternatives, meaning non-UCITS. In addition a special regime was added for real estate funds, the ELTIFs (European long-term investment funds).

In this chapter, we start with a review of the changes in the EU's asset management markets as a result of the crisis. A second part discusses the new regulatory framework for asset management and the challenges ahead. We focus primarily on the new AIFMD, the consolidation of the UCITS regime and its recent changes, and challenges ahead. We make reference to the links with other regulatory frameworks, primarily Solvency II and the markets in financial instruments Directive (MiFID) as necessary.

3.1 The asset management industry

The crisis fundamentally altered the face of the asset management industry, allowing the insurance industry to re-emerge as the leading player. Of the three traditional groups of institutional investors – investment funds, insurance companies and pension funds – the first group had dominated the sector in terms of total assets since 2004. But the financial crisis led to big outflows and declines in value in investment funds, which only gradually recovered. By the end of 2014, net assets under management (AuM) by the European industry totalled €19.0 trillion, representing a 39.7% increase compared to the end of 2007, when they totalled €13.6 trillion. Discretionary mandates' assets at the end of 2014 were estimated at €9.9 trillion, or 52% of AuM, whereas investment funds accounted for the remaining €9.1 trillion or 48% of AuM – of which about 71% or €6.5 trillion are long-term UCITS, that is, UCITS excluding money market funds.

Figure 2. Total AuM of the European asset management industry (investment funds and discretionary mandates) by client type (€ trillion)

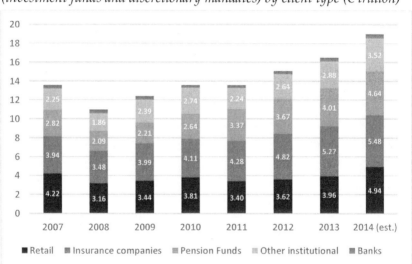

Source: Author's own elaboration based on data from EFAMA.

By client type, the insurers' assets in the EU has increased in value from 3.9 € trillion in 2007 to an estimated €5.5 trillion in 2014, while financial assets of pension funds totalled €4.6 trillion in the same year, up from €2.8 trillion in 2007. The retail clients share grew the least, which raises some fiduciary duty issues, as discussed below.

Although some insurance companies and pension funds manage assets in-house, a substantial number of these firms rely on the expertise of third-party asset managers. In some cases, they may adopt a hybrid model, keeping some investment functions in-house while outsourcing others. For example, at year-end 2013, around 67% of the insurers' investment portfolio was managed by third-party asset managers compared to 33% that was managed in-house.

The dramatic decline in the European investment fund industry in 2008 reflected the extraordinary events in financial markets following the fall of Lehman Brothers, with huge declines in global stock markets, big outflows of money out of the financial system and out of equity investment funds in particular. In the retail space, the loss on confidence in managers was coupled with extended sovereign guarantees on bank deposits, prompting a flight to safety. This decline was prolonged in Europe as a result of the sovereign debt crisis, which led to a repatriation of assets and a restoration of the home bias. This trend only started to be reversed in the second half of 2012. By comparison, the European insurance industry, which also manages long-term savings plans in life insurance products and group insurance plans, but on its balance sheet, managed to consolidate its image as a truly long-term institutional investor.

The growth of the European and US fund industry was fairly comparable until the crisis struck, but the decline was more pronounced in the EU, and the recovery in the US. Assets managed by the EU and US funds stood at 31% and 57%, respectively, of worldwide assets in the third quarter of 2014 (ICI, 2014).

Events in financial markets had a direct bearing on the investment fund industry and on its future structure. The demise of Lehman Brothers revealed the uncertainty of holdings trapped in bankruptcy procedures and the non-market risks linked to the use of derivatives. Some banks had also made use of structured products, such as collateralised debt obligations (CDOs) to support guaranteed equity products. The large-scale fraud perpetrated by Bernard Madoff, blown wide open by the end of 2008, was a further setback for the fund industry, which revealed the shortcomings prevalent in the regulation of custody and the need for action at global level. Several European managers had invested in Madoff funds (mostly through funds of funds or feeder structures) but had not taken proper measures to ensure a complete separation between fund manager and depositary, as required under UCITS. Industry and regulators suddenly woke up to counterparty and custody risks in asset management.

The decline in the European fund industry emphasised even more the need for further consolidation, as the average size per fund declined. The average size of a UCITS today is seven times that of an average US mutual fund, although the 10% largest funds concentrate 65% of assets (Lannoo, 2015). The sub-optimal average UCITS size brings about higher operational costs for investment management, a high total expense ratio (TER) or management fee for the investor and duplication of infrastructure. In this sense, the European asset management industry still today performs below its potential, the cost of which is passed on to the user. The main causes are to be found in the high level of fragmentation, the absence of a European market concept among investors and firms, and the remunerative niche markets that funds can target, exploiting differences in tax and regulatory regimes across Europe. The UCITS IV amendments, discussed below, address these challenges, but only partially. Another revision of the Directive is expected to further remove barriers to market integration.

The long-term implications of the financial crisis for the fund industry remain unchanged. Too many funds were too closely managed or distributed by deposit-taking banks as an alternative savings instrument. Even today most funds are distributed by banks in Europe – a situation that poses questions in terms of competition and market structure. The situation persists, despite the recent growth in passive and exchange-traded investing, the development of alternative distribution platforms and the forced sales of asset management subsidiaries by several banks in Europe, following the financial crisis and the conditions linked to state aid. Measures need to be elaborated to support the separation between banks and fund managers and to come to a more genuine application of the open architecture framework. This calls, inter alia, for a stricter application of conflict of interest rules, as enshrined in MiFID I and II. In particular, it raises the question whether the cost of investment advice needs to be fully separated from management fees, as is required in the UK and the Netherlands.

3.2 The UCITS regime

UCITS accounts today for almost a third of global assets in traditional investment funds, a quarter of which are sourced outside Western Europe. With changes in the course of implementation and others still in the pipeline, the UCITS regime has reached a high degree of maturity, but at the same time complexity. UCITS IV allows greater market integration for the fund industry, UCITS V adds some elements of the AIFMD to UCITS, mainly as regards the separation between depositary and fund manager, and the remuneration of fund managers. Amidst growing recognition that the UCITS framework needs a full recast to achieve modernisation and simplification, the European Commission launched a consultation in 2012. The future UCITS VI framework may take the form of a regulation and address the use of derivatives and indices, leverage limits and access to less-liquid asset classes.

The UCITS framework is one of the bright stories of European integration but the single market for UCITS funds remains evasive, given the lack of progress at EU level in addressing the distribution and infrastructure bottlenecks. Member states are adopting their own solutions, addressing in particular conflicts of interest in retail distribution, building sensible but divergent frameworks that act as barriers to the cross-border business. The situation is unlikely to be solved unless EU standards would converge to the highest national denominator.

The 1985 UCITS Directive was the frontrunner of a wave of EU rules governing the free provision of financial services across borders under home country rules. The Directive introduced harmonised *product* regulation for investment funds that were allowed for cross-border sales in the EU (and the countries of the European Economic Area). It was followed in the early 1990s with directives defining the terms under which the banking, insurance and investment services sectors could 'passport' their *services* across the EU on the basis of authorisation from their home-state regulator (see Table 2 below).

Table 2. Salient aspects of EU financial services directives affecting the asset management business

	Capital Requirements Directive (CRD IV)	Solvency II	Pension Funds Directive (IORP)	MiFID II	UCITS III, IV and V	Alternative investment funds managers (AIFs)
Initial capital	- Minimum €5 million	- Minimum capital requirement or MCR	- Capital depends on the sort of guarantee (if any) provided to beneficiaries and the presence of steering mechanisms (under upcoming revision of directive)	- Minimum €730,000, may be reduced to €125,000 for not for own account trading firms, or €50,000 for local firms (Directive 2013/36/EU, CRD IV)	- €125,000 per management company - Plus 0.02% of AuM exceeding €250m - Max. €10m capital	- €300,000 for internally managed AIFM or €125,000 for externally managed AIFM+ - Plus 0.02% of AuM exceeding €250m - Max. €10m capital
Additional capital requirements	- Minimum 8% (tier 1 and 2) of risk-weighted assets or VAR for trading book, systemic and buffers	- Solvency capital requirement of SCR - Risk-based solvency charges based on standard formula or approved internal models	- Risk-based solvency charges (under upcoming revision of directive)	- Function of trading book (Directive 2013/36/EU (CRD IV) and Regulation 575/2013 (CRR))	- Capital requirement shall never be less than required under Art. 21 of Directive 2006/49/EC	- Capital requirement shall never be less than required under Art. 21 of Directive 2006/49/EC
Permissible activities (non-exhaustive, only when related to	- Portfolio management, safekeeping and administration of	- Life insurance (including group insurance)	- Management and investment of funded	- Individual portfolio management, securities	- Management of investment funds - Non-core:	- Management and marketing of non-UCITS - EU AIFMs

… asset management)	securities, trading in and underwriting of securities	Non-life insurance (large and mass risk)	occupational pension schemes	brokerage and order execution activities	Discretionary asset management (including pension funds), Investment advice, Safekeeping (custody) and administration of UCITS	Non-EU AIFMs if they manage an EU AIF or market a non-EU AIF in EU
Asset allocation	- Holdings in non-financial institutions limited to 60% of own funds, and 15% for a single holding. - Large credit exposures to single clients are limited to 800% of own funds and 25% for a single exposure	- Quantitative restrictions abolished by Solvency II, and replaced by a risk-based regime	- Investment limits based on minimum harmonisation - Member states may set more stringent rules for institutions active on their territory, but within certain limits; - Investment in sponsoring undertaking are limited to 5% of the technical provisions	- Rules on large exposures	- < 10% of assets in single security, except for public debt, and < 40% for single investments of 5% - < 10% non-listed securities - < 10% of same body for money market instruments, and < 20% for investments in single other funds and deposits with credit institutions - Special rules for master-feeder structures	- No requirements - Liquidity towards investors in line with liquidity of underlying - Special reporting requirements to supervisors for certain leveraged AIFs
Conduct of business	- Host-country rules on advertising and 'general good'	- Responsibility and governance - Conflicts of interest - Conduct of business specific	- Conflicts of interest - Host country social and labour rules	- Harmonised, but host country in charge of enforcement of rules for branches	- Host country conduct of business rules (unless subject to MiFID rules for non-core);	- Conflict of interest - Risk and portfolio management functions

Disclosure	- Pillar III	to life and non-life activities - Valuation - Public disclosure - Disclosure to supervisors - Disclosure to clients	- Disclosure of investment policies, risk and accrued benefits to fund members	- Extensive, full price transparency (equity securities, fixed income, commodities), unbundling of cost of transactions	- Host country advertising and marketing rules - Key Investor Information Document (KIID)	- Delegation and outsourcing - Valuation - Remuneration - Annual report, disclosure of investment strategy, risk management, depository, fees and charges - Reporting to authorities - Controlling stake notification rules
Investor compensation	- Deposit guarantee Directive			- Investor compensation schemes directive	- Investor compensation schemes (depending upon national implementation)	- Not applicable
Final date for implementation	- 2014	- New framework (Solvency II) by 2014	- 2004	- November 2007/2016	- July 2011 (UCITS IV), 2016 (UCITS V)	- July 2013
Technical adaptations	- European Banking Committee (EBC), extensive	- European Insurance and Occupational Pensions Committee, extensive	- European Insurance and Occupational Pensions Committee, limited	- European Securities Committee (ESC), extensive	- European Securities Committee (ESC), limited	- European Securities Committee (ESC), extensive

The UCITS Directive was amended and expanded in 2002 and again in 2009, to become more of a horizontal asset management directive to reflect the increasing convergence of the core sectors of the financial services industry, and in 2014, to clarify the delegation arrangements and the depositaries' liability. The last sector to undergo cross-border liberalisation was pension funds in 2002. The Directive on Institutions for Occupational Retirement Provision (IORPs) had limited success so far – there were only 11 cross-border IORPs in Europe in 2011 – and is now being revised to tighten supervision and governance arrangements for funds. In the meantime, the new wave of the Financial Services Action Plan (FSAP) had started to come into effect, most importantly with MiFID. In 2012, the AIFMD came to set the framework for all non-UCITS managers in the pursuit of a level-playing field and more transparency towards both supervisors and investors.

The UCITS framework itself has been transformed over time. In 2002, key amendments expanded the scope of activities that were possible under the original UCITS Directive. The so-called 'UCITS III' product directive widened the scope of eligible assets for funds, to include derivatives and indices, under certain conditions. It also facilitated new formats, such as funds of funds, money market funds, cash funds or index tracker funds. A second directive – the UCITS III Management Directive – detailed minimum standards, including the introduction of a minimum level of own funds to be held by the management company and broadened its permissible activities. It also introduced a simplified prospectus, the predecessor of today's key investor information document (KIID). The UCITS III Directive granted the 'single license' to fund management companies in the broad sense of the word. It comprises not only the management of investment funds – the core services – but also other activities related to portfolio management, such as pension funds for individuals, investment advice and administration of investment funds, which are seen as non-core or ancillary.[30]

---

[30] Other forms of portfolio management, e.g. management of pension fund portfolios or those of individuals, are presented as a derogation from the central objective of the Directive, which is management of investment funds as authorised under the Directive (Art. 5).

In 2009, at the depth of the financial crisis, UCITS IV brought forth a further set of amendments, which had to be implemented by July 2011. These facilitated a genuine European passport for UCITS management companies, allowing for the separation between the location of the company and the jurisdiction where funds are registered. UCITS IV also facilitates cross-border mergers of UCITS, which makes it possible to increase the average size of European funds. In the same vein, it allows for master-feeder structures, which had previously been specifically excluded due to concerns over portfolio diversification.[31] Entity pooling should generate scale economies and thus contribute to a consolidation of the sector serving end-users. However, the uptake has been limited so far, since barriers remain, notably with respect to taxation. Finally, UCITS IV further eases cross-border marketing of UCITS by simplifying administrative procedures. The home supervisor directly notifies the host authorities, which can monitor commercial documents but cannot refuse access.

UCITS has also served as a laboratory for EU investor protection, in particular for disclosure rules. UCITS IV created the first EU standard format of summary pre-contractual disclosure. The 'key investor information document' or KIID was an important step forward in helping consumers choose and understand their purchases. It is currently being reviewed in the context of its extension to other (packaged) retail and insurance-linked investment products (PRIIPs). The new standard should help to compare UCITS with other investments such as unit-linked insurance policies, personal pensions and bank structured products, but the challenge of comparability should not be underestimated.

Yet, the investor protection credentials of UCITS suffered a great blow with the Madoff scandal. In response, the European Commission proposed a stricter separation between the depositary or custodian and the fund manager. Madoff revealed that parts of the European asset managers had not properly applied the separation between manager and depositary, which is a strict obligation under UCITS. The scandal also highlighted that the UCITS rules on deposits were only principle-based and had not

---

[31] A 'feeder UCITS' is a UCITS or an investment compartment thereof that invests at least 85% of its assets in another UCITS, called the 'master UCITS'.

been correctly implemented in several EU member states (ESMA, 2010). The issue is also that once certain derivative financial instruments are allowed to be used in UCITS, a 100% separate holding certainty is illusory since derivatives cannot be held in custody as transferable securities can. The UCITS V Directive (adopted in 2014) brings the depositary rules in UCITS in line with those in the AIFMD. In addition, it adds rules regarding the remuneration of fund managers, as was also included in the AIFMD.

The duties of fund depositaries in EU regulation boil down to three: i) control the title of any assets received by the fund; ii) keep assets in custody or, where this is not possible, keep their records; and iii) monitor cash flows and other oversight functions. The difference between *custody* and *record-keeping* is fundamental, given the different standards of responsibility that apply. Custody involves holding a security, either physically or electronically while record-keeping only concerns taking note of the given right or contract. The AIFMD imposes strict liability for the loss of an asset kept in custody while liability in record-keeping arises in case of negligence or intentional failure. The gist is in determining which assets can be *kept in custody* instead of *kept in record.* Only transferable securities, money market instruments and fund units capable of being held in an account in the name of the depository can be held in custody. Less clear cut is the situation arising in cases of collateral arrangements, securities lending and repos. The assets exit custody only if there is a transfer of ownership away from the alternative fund manager.

Therefore, each transaction needs to be examined. Indeed, the 2002 collateral Directive distinguishes between 'title transfer' and 'security' arrangements: under a security arrangement there is no transfer of title so the assets remain in custody. But without harmonised securities and bankruptcy laws, problems will continue to arise in practice. The key difference between the depositary rules for UCITS and AIFs lies in the ability of (professional) investors in AIFs to renounce some of the guarantees offered by the Directive (in relation to the restitution of lost assets) in a limited number of circumstances, catering in particular for investments in emerging economies.

3.3   A new EU regime for 'alternative' funds

The financial crisis crystallised the consensus that European and global regulation of alternative funds was necessary. Before 2008, regulatory approaches varied across European jurisdictions, from registration-only to more detailed frameworks. The crisis changed this view rapidly, and although initially much politicised and strongly contested by the industry, the new regime is now seen as an opportunity for business growth, as like for UCITS, a single passport now exists for alternative fund managers in the EU, albeit restricted to professional clients.

The London G-20 summit in April 2009 agreed that "all systemically important financial institutions, markets and instruments should be subject to an appropriate degree of regulation and oversight". Leaders of the world's main economies intended to put an end to regulatory arbitrage, seen to be one of the drivers of the crisis. The G-20 stated that hedge funds and other asset managers should be registered and disclose information about their leverage to supervisors. In addition, they should be subject to effective risk management.

The AIFMD proposal was under preparation before the crisis broke and was published very soon after the London G-20. The problem was to find a comprehensive way of regulating the sector, given its diversity and the risk of relocation to offshore jurisdictions. The EU Directive applies to managers of alternative investment funds – wherever they are registered – and formally not to the funds. In contrast with UCITS, the AIFMD does not contain product structuring rules, such as restrictions on eligible assets, issuer concentration or leverage limits. In this sense, and by adding a reciprocity provision, the EU ensures that the whole non-harmonised fund sector that falls outside the scope of the UCITS Directive is covered, including also private equity, commodity and real estate funds. Managers of funds domiciled in third countries will be able to benefit from the EU passport after an uncertain transition period, provided they comply with the Directive (de Manuel & Lannoo, 2012, p. 95 and Annex 2).

The AIFMD Directive follows to a great extent the spirit of the provisions in UCITS and MiFID on the conduct of business, organisational, reporting and prudential requirements. The

Directive added elements that have come up in the crisis, such as the need for appropriate liquidity management, strict segregation of assets and additional reporting requirements for highly leveraged funds. It adopts a tough stance on delegation and outsourcing to limit circumvention.

The AIFMD applies a partial exemption to managers under €100 million assets under management or €500 million if investors are locked in for five years and in the absence of leverage. Managers under this threshold will be requested to register and provide simplified reporting to authorities to enable more effective financial stability oversight. The transparency threshold for private equity managers with stakes in non-listed companies is 10% for disclosure to competent authorities and over 50% of voting rights for disclosure to other shareholders.

Although intensely criticised by the industry, which claimed it would lead to high costs for investors and a flight of funding activities out of the EU, the Directive creates a single licence for non-UCITS funds and their managers in the EU, which had not existed before. In sum, the AIFMD represents a consistent framework for the regulation of the wider asset management industry from a prudential policy perspective by introducing minimum common rules. In particular, it addresses: i) prudential oversight, ii) leverage and pro-cyclicality, iii) maturity and liquidity transformation and iv) links with the banking system. It is also aimed at improving transparency and service obligations towards professional investors but relies on the buy-side prudential rules to enforce full transparency on the underlying (the look-through principle in Solvency II). More clarity within the non-UCITS sector will benefit users, supervisors and the industry alike.

With the agreement reached on the European long-term investment funds (ELTIFs) in April 2015, an EU-wide product regime now also exists for illiquid assets, such as real estate, infrastructure and unlisted securities. But only managers authorised under the AIFMD can offer ELTIFs. Unlike UCITS, ELTIFS are not redeemable whenever the investor wishes; on the contrary. Investors in ELTIFs will usually only be able to withdraw money at the specified end date of their investment, at least ten years after the initial payment is made. Withdrawing money earlier can be done, on the condition that certain criteria are met. Although the product is mostly designed for institutional investors, investment is also possible by retail investors. Details will have to be worked out in implementing legislation.

3.4 Money market funds

By most accounts, money market funds (MMFs) were the worst affected sector in the asset management industry by the financial crisis. The run on US money market funds in 2008 underlined not only their importance for the economy but also the lack of any specific EU framework for MMFs other than UCITS. Divergent national requirements allowed the use of the denomination 'money market' for funds with constant and fluctuating net asset values (NAVs), funds investing in longer maturities and even funds investing in non-money market instruments (usually called cash+funds). In stark contrast, US MMFs were narrowly defined by the Investment Company Act of 1940 (2a-7 rule) as stable-NAV complying with specific requirements on credit quality and maturity, among others.

The European Securities and Markets Authority (ESMA) issued guidelines in 2010 on the common definition of MMFs in the EU. It introduced two categories of money market funds: i) *short-term MMFs* subject to the same maturity constraints as MMFs in the US, after the 2010 revision of the 2a-7 rule; and ii) MMFs invested in longer-term securities under a fluctuating NAV.

Stable-NAV MMFs are at the centre of the international discussions on 'shadow banking' led by the Financial Stability Board (FSB). It was proposed that the constant NAV MMFs would have either to provide sufficient capital to back their 'promise' of liquidity at face value or otherwise completely abandon such 'promise' and move into fluctuating NAVs. But fierce opposition by the industry, coupled with the fear of causing stress in money markets, have frustrated reform by the SEC so far. The stable NAV associated with US MMFs is not prevalent in Europe where even 'short-term MMFs' tend to have fluctuating NAVs. The European Commission proposed to implement the FSB guidelines in September 2013 with a regulation on money market funds, i.e. constant NAV can only be promised if funds have a capital buffer of at least 3%. The European Parliament proposed to allow constant NAVs without capital buffer for MMF invested government securities, and for MMFs bought by public authorities, charities and NGOs. It will be up to the EU Council and the European Parliament to reach agreement on this.

3.5   The interaction with MiFID

Whereas UCITS, strictly speaking, regulates products and the AIFMD managers, MiFID regulates investment services, affecting the wider asset management industry but also the insurance sector. It allows for the free provision of investment services all over the EU with a single licence, subject to conduct-of-business and organisational provisions. The 2004 MiFID was replaced by MiFID II and MiFIR (markets in financial Instruments Regulation) in 2014, extending the scope and considerably tightening the rules. The challenge for the industry is how to deal with the interaction between these three pieces of legislation.

MiFID brought more competition to exchanges in equity trading, by abolishing their monopoly, and through the introduction of alternative trading facilities. In return, it imposed stricter requirements on firms in securities transactions, through best execution, client categorisation (the 'suitability' and 'appropriateness' test), conflict-of-interest and transaction reporting requirements, which have been harmonised to a high degree. These measures reduced transaction costs, but the benefits to users have so far failed to materialise (Valiante & Lannoo, 2011). MiFID II further tightens the rules, but will only be fully applicable by 2017.

Conduct-of-business rules in MiFID apply to asset managers when they provide discretionary asset management and investment advice, as well as to the providers of back-office services such as custody and administration. MiFID applies therefore to product originators, in this instance fund managers, to the extent that they also carry out the distribution of their products. These rules are above all organisational requirements, in particular regarding the prevention of conflicts of interest, and conduct-of-business obligations, in particular client suitability and best execution.

An important issue for the fund management industry is the regime for inducements under MiFID. Inducements are payments by an investment firm of a fee, commission or non-monetary benefit that could place the firm in a situation where it would not be acting in compliance with the MiFID principle of acting "honestly, fairly and professionally in accordance with the best interest of clients" (Art. 24 MiFID II). The initial MiFID rules required distributors to demonstrate that inducements paid by the originator did not result in bias and facilitated enhanced services for customers. The difficulties in enforcing this approach in practice, in the context of the fallout from the financial crisis, were driving the revision of the directive, as discussed below.

In effect, conflict-of-interest provisions create difficulties for widely accepted distribution practices in the fund management industry, namely the retrocession of fees from originators to distributors. In some instances product providers and intermediaries may be contemplating significant fees as a condition for the products being placed on the distributor's panel or recommended list. Such fees are unconnected with, and additional to, conventional commissions which are paid on the sale of particular products. They are thus incompatible with the fundamental principle that a firm must not conduct business under arrangements in conflict with fiduciary duties to customers.

Following the financial crisis, MiFID was opened for review in 2011, focusing on the upgrade of the conduct-of-business provisions and extending the requirements for trading facilities. It concerned the extension of the pre-trade price transparency provisions to the non-equity markets, particularly bond and derivative markets and the clarification of the rules applicable to in-house matching by investment banks ('dark pools'). To better ensure accurate implementation, these elements are part of a regulation (MiFIR), whereas the organisational and conduct-of-business rules for trading platforms, brokers and data vendors are part of an update to the directive (MiFID II). Thus, the most important changes take the form of tighter rules for investment advice in order to better protect investors in the sale of complex financial products. Investment advice should be provided to clients on an independent basis; hence inducements are banned and fees must be unbundled (Art. 24 MiFID II).

The label for independent advisors and the disclosure of the costs linked to distribution should help investors make more informed decisions, but questions concerning quality of advice and professional standards remain. Some member states have adopted bolder structural solutions to conflicts of interest in distribution (notably a complete separation between sales and advice), but EU legislation did not follow suit. In the absence of structural solutions, much will depend on the effective application of the Directive in practice. Many blame poor supervision for the dismal record of MiFID I in improving investor protection. The new supervisory set-up, discussed below, is expected to improve the situation.

MiFID II is also expected to address the increasing complexity of some UCITS funds, following the expansion of eligible assets and practices enabled by UCITS III in 2009. Under MiFID I, all UCITS benefit from a blank categorisation as 'non-complex' financial instruments. This means that UCITS can be sold without any intermediary assessment of the adequacy of the product to the individual investor. This so-called 'execution only' regime is an exception to the generally applicable MiFID suitability and appropriateness tests. The growing complexity of UCITS products has challenged this exception: The evidence that investors do not understand non-market risks (such as counterparty risk) embedded in the use of derivatives calls for a cautionary approach in the sale process. Most retail investors purchasing an 'investment fund' still expect to hold the underlying securities and would need professional advice to understand, for instance, the benefits and risks of accessing the returns of the same basket of securities through a total return swap. But the question remains whether the issue should be tackled by reforming MiFID or UCITS itself.

Product proliferation within UCITS has rendered its future uncertain, in particular after the adoption of AIFMD. Much bespoke brand fragmentation is already a reality. Not only do markets refer to 'alternative UCITS', but the UCITS rules themselves distinguish categories of UCITS such as sophisticated, structured, exchange-traded and money-market. The introduction of the AIFMD as a horizontal legislation for all non-UCITS managers has increased the pressure to restrict the UCITS brand to traditional practices.

3.6   Impact of the changing supervisory set-up

The financial crisis finally made the Europeans realise that the form of supervisory cooperation they had was not adequate for their degree of market integration. Under the new set-up, supervision is much more coordinated, with the implementation of conduct-of-business rules being monitored by the European Securities Markets Authority (ESMA), and prudential control of banks almost entirely in the hands of the European Central Bank under the single supervisory mechanism. How the interaction between both will work in the future remains to be seen.

The financial crisis revealed serious shortcomings in the oversight of financial markets, which initially led to the recommendations contained in the 2009 de Larosière report, and later in 2012 to the calls for a full Banking Union. The de Larosière report created the European System of Financial Supervisors (ESFS), comprising three functional authorities covering banking, insurance and securities markets, and a European Systemic Risk Board (ESRB), administered by the ECB. These authorities have the formal responsibility to enforce EU rules and supervise its application by national supervisors, and should thus contribute to eliminate some of the problems raised above. The ultimate goal is to have a single rulebook, which means having exactly the same rules in all member states across the Union. A single rulebook is also the objective of the ECB's single supervisory mechanism, although it is too early to judge how this will work in practice.

In the field of asset management, the responsibilities reside clearly in the field of ESMA, whose role has not been questioned as a result of the sovereign crisis. ESMA has the formal responsibility to mediate between supervisory authorities, and to delegate supervisory powers in the supervision of fund managers, for example. The role of ESMA appears of particular importance in providing technical guidance to the Commission to implement the post-crisis legislation and set standards, relying on supervisory coordination mechanisms and using powers of direct intervention only in exceptional circumstances.

3.7 Towards a horizontal asset management regime

A comparison of various national regimes within the EU covering retail investment products reveals an immense diversity, with a patchwork of different obligations on distributors regarding disclosure and investor protection, different forms of prudential supervision and a high degree of variation in marketing and advertising rules (see Table 3). The major challenge for the years to come is to work out a coherent regime for retail investment products across sectors at EU level. The 2012 initiative on packaged retail investment products (PRIPs) aimed to level the playing field from the perspective of information and distribution. It was extended to insurance products and culminated in the adoption of the packaged retail investment and insurance-based products Regulation (PRIIP) in December 2014, to be applicable from 2017 onwards.

From a prudential perspective, diverse business models and promises to investors warrant distinct treatment. Guaranteed insurance products are to be based on capital requirements (per Solvency II) while non-guaranteed products, where the full market risk falls on the investor, barely need any capital backing. Examples of the latter are investment funds and defined contribution pensions. Defined benefit pensions and hybrid arrangements will be subject to distinct rules that will take into account the promises made to beneficiaries and the steering mechanisms available, including the ability to raise contributions, cut benefits or rely on sponsor support. These changes will be operated under a revised Directive on Institutions for Occupational Retirement Provision (IORPs). No framework exists yet in Europe for third-pillar pensions but the European Commission asked EIOPA in 2012 to deliver technical advice by 2015 – a process on which the future of the European asset management industry largely depends.

Product structuring and authorisation rules remain very much fragmented, despite the fact that the similar economic functions of retail products called for a consistent approach. Until recently, unit-linked insurance products were not subject to EU rules on structuring while bank-structured products are even less regulated. The introduction into MiFID II of so-called 'suitability at product design' could provide the basis for a uniform framework based on the responsibility of senior management to approve the policy governing the services and products offered by the firm, in accordance with the characteristics and needs of the clients to whom their products will be offered or provided (see Art. 9). The extension of this principle to insurance products (in the Insurance Mediation Directive or IMD) and its practical implementation is now part of the PRIIPS Regulation.

As for distribution, the level of mandatory fiduciary care afforded to retail investors as well as the degree of supervision undertaken by regulatory authorities may vary depending on the distribution channel through which they access investment products, even if, in terms of outcomes or payoff profiles, the products are broadly similar. Pre-contractual disclosure is harmonised in the form of a mandatory key investor information document (KIID) for investment funds, unit-linked insurance policies, structured products and third-pillar retirement schemes under the PRIIPS Regulation. Plain vanilla securities have to comply with the Prospectus Directive. Sales practices are governed by MiFID II except for unit-linked insurance products, which will remain under the IMD. As for private placements, MiFID will continue to apply to the extent that the securities are placed via investment firms in the sense indicated in the Directive (banks, brokers or financial advisers).

Table 3. EU regulatory framework for retail investment products

		Product				
		UCITS	**Non-UCITS (AIFs)**	**Life insurance (also unit-linked)**	**Listed security**	**Structured products**
Framework	**Marketing and sales practices**	- MiFID - UCITS - PRIIPs (2019)	- MiFID - AIFMD - PRIIPs (retail) - ELTIF	- IMD - PRIIPs	- MiFID	- MiFID - PRIIPs
		Distance Marketing of Financial Services Directive				
	Disclosure	- PRIIPs (2019) - UCITS - MiFID	- PRIIPs (retail) - AIFMD - MiFID - ELTIF	- PRIIPs - Solvency II - IMD	- Prospectus directive	- PRIIPs - MiFID
	Asset allocation	- UCITS	- ELTIF	- UCITS (unit-linked)		
	Prudential	- UCITS	- AIFMD	- Solvency II		- CRD IV

Source: Author's own compilation.

In view of the above, the framework for investment products remains very complex, even for an informed investor. Some products are tightly regulated at EU level, whereas for others, there is only general service-level rules. The problems raised by the interaction of a product directive (e.g. UCITS) with the rest of the framework (not based on product rules) indicates that many questions remain to be answered, possibly by developing a strong set of product-to-market principles and supervision, based on the responsibility of the originator to design products generally suitable for the investors they target.

The PRIIPS Regulation, which has to be applied from 2017 onwards, can bring more alignment in the applicable marketing and sales practices for retail investment products, by making the KIID obligatory. Whether this will effectively be the case remains to be seen, as the KIID is already required for UCITS today, which is not necessarily effectively implemented. It will be up to the member states, and the European Supervisory Authorities (ESAs), to ensure consistent implementation. The latter can prohibit the marketing, distribution or sale of certain products in certain circumstances. It is hoped that a more consistent regime for retail investment products will eventually emerge in future, and that the interaction with other pieces legislation, such as MiFID II, can be streamlined.

3.8   Conclusions

A well-developed regulatory framework is in place for the asset management industry in the European Union. Two basic regimes are emerging, one for retail investment products under UCITS and a second one under the AIFMD for professional investors. This has levelled the playing field between both. At the same time, the more integrated EU supervisory structure should lead to a stricter enforcement of rules, most notably with regard to the conduct of business rules enshrined in MiFID, and for marketing and distribution rules in PRIIPs. But much remains still to be done to bring full coherence to these frameworks.

Post-crisis, the challenge for the industry and policy-makers is to restore confidence and allow a re-diversification of the savings of households. As further to the financial crisis, the increase in the protection offered by deposit guarantee schemes and the government bail-out of the banking system resulted in a concentration of savings in the banking sector. This is however an unhealthy situation, as much for households as for the economy as a whole, since the transfer of savings to productive investments is hindered. The asset management industry should furthermore strive to deliver long-term value opportunities to investors, looking beyond UCITS into balanced funds for retirement savings.

In the medium to long run, the objective should be to create a more coherent framework for the retail investment product regime across sectors and for long-term investments. Too many differences remain in the rules applicable to the fund business and other product originators, despite the recent initiatives. This creates distortions of competition, but also leads to inefficiencies and maintains the vertical structure of the financial industry as we know it today. A more open architecture of the financial industry should be the imperative across the board, in the interest of consumers and the public at large.

References and selected bibliography

BCG (2011), "Global Asset Management 2011: Building on Success", Boston Consulting Group, Boston, MA.

Casey, Jean-Pierre and Karel Lannoo (2009), *Pouring old wine in new skins? UCITS and Asset Management after MiFID*, CEPS Paperback, Centre for European Policy Studies, Brussels.

Clifford Chance (2015), "The PRIIPs KID Regime", March.

de Larosière, J., L. Balcerowicz, O. Issing, R. Masera, C.M. Carthy, L. Nyberg, J. Pérez et al. (2009), "Report of the High-Level Group on Financial Supervision in the EU", Brussels.

de Manuel Aramendía, M.J. and Karel Lannoo (2012), *Rethinking Asset Management: From Financial Stability to Investor Protection and Economic Growth*, CEPS-ECMI Task Force Report, European Capital Markets Institute and Centre for European Policy Studies, Brussels.

de Manuel Aramendía, M.J. (2010), "Third Country Rules for Alternative Investments: Passport flexibility comes at a price", ECMI Commentaries, 16 December, European Capital Markets Institute, Brussels.

_____ (2012b), "Will the PRIPs' KID live up to its promise to protect investors?", ECMI Commentary, 6 July, European Capital Markets Institute, Brussels.

de Manuel Aramendía, M.J. and Diego Valiente (2014), "A Life Cycle Approach to Investor Protection", ECMI Working Paper, European Capital Markets Institute, Brussels, September.

ECB (2011), Statistical Data Warehouse, European Central Bank, Frankfurt.

EFAMA (2011), *Asset Management in Europe: Facts and Figures*, European Fund and Asset Management Association, Brussels.

ESMA (2009), *Guidelines on a Common Definition of European Money Market Funds*, CESR/10-049, European Securities and Markets Authority, Paris.

_____ (2010), Mapping of duties and liabilities of UCITS depositaries, CESR/09-175, European Securities and Markets Authority, Paris.

_____ (2012), Guidelines on ETFs and other UCITS Issues, ESMA 2012/474, European Securities and Markets Authority, Paris.

EIWG (European Investors Working Group) (2010), "Restoring Investor Confidence in European Capital Markets", European Capital Markets Institute (ECMI), Brussels.

European Commission (2006), White Paper on Enhancing the Single Market Framework for Investment Funds, COM (2006) 686 final, European Commission, Brussels.

_____ (2009), Communication on Packaged Retail Investment Products, COM (2009) 204 final, European Commission, Brussels.

_____ (2012a), Consultation on Undertakings for Collective Investment in Transferable Securities (UCITS) with respect to Product Rules, Liquidity Management, Depositary, Money Market Funds and Long-term Investments, 26 July 2012, European Commission, Brussels.

_____ (2012b), Proposal for a Directive amending Directive 2009/65/EC on the coordination of laws, regulations and administrative provisions relating to undertakings for collective investment in transferable securities (UCITS) as regards depositary functions, remuneration policies and sanctions (UCITS V), COM(2012) 350 final, European Commission, Brussels.

FSA (2009), Distribution of retail investments: Delivering the RDR, Consultation Paper 09/18, Financial Services Authority, London.

_____ (2011a), "Shadow Banking: Strengthening Oversight and Regulation", October, Financial Stability Board, Basel.

_____ (2011b), "Shadow Banking: Scoping the Issues", Financial Stability Board, Basel.

ICI (2011), "Investment Company Fact Book", Investment Company Institute, Washington, D.C.

_____ (2014), "Worldwide Mutual Fund Assets and Flows", Third Quarter 2014, Investment Company Institute, Washington, D.C.

Insurance Europe (2012), "The European Life Insurance Market in 2010", European Insurance and Reinsurance Federation, Brussels.

Lannoo, Karel (2015), Which Union for Europe's Capital Markets, ECMI Policy Brief No. 22, Brussels, February.

Moody's (2010), "Sponsor Support Key to Money Market Funds", Moody's Investor Service.

OECD (2011), "Fostering Long-term Investment and Economic Growth: A Long-term Investor's View", Financial Market Trends, 2011(1), pp. 1-4, Organisation for Economic Co-operation and Development, Paris.

OEE (2011), "The Importance of Asset Management to the European Economy", Observatoire de l'Eparge Européene, Paris.

PWGFM (2010), "Money Market Fund Reform Options", US President's Working Group on Financial Markets.

SEC (2011), Use of Derivatives by Investment Companies Under the Investment Company Act of 1940, Securities and Exchange Commission, Release No. IC-29776, File No. S7-33-11, Washington, D.C.

Valiante, D. and K. Lannoo (2011), MiFID 2.0 Casting New Light on Europe's Capital Markets, CEPS-ECMI Paperback, Centre for European Policy Studies and European Capital Markets Institute, Brussels.

4. SOLIDIFYING DERIVATIVES MARKETS AND FINANCIAL INFRASTRUCTURE*

In line with the G-20 commitment, a large part of the over-the-counter (OTC) derivatives market moved to central clearing fairly rapidly. The reaction created a clear trend break and brought the uncontrolled growth of the market, at least measured as notional amounts outstanding, to an end. Implementation is still in progress and continues to provoke tensions, mostly between the two blocs, the EU and the US, whose banks control a large chunk of this market.

The move to require central trading and clearing of trades in derivatives followed failures in non-collateralised positions in bilateral OTC derivatives trading, mainly with the US group AIG, but also with other financial institutions. These failures sparked systemic disruption across the globe and led to a costly bailout for US taxpayers in 2008. The need for effective safeguards to deal with counterparty risks in derivatives trading was a key element in both the London and Pittsburgh G-20 meetings. The Pittsburgh G-20 decided that "all standardized OTC derivative contracts should be traded on exchanges or electronic trading platforms, where appropriate, and cleared through central counterparties (CCPs) by the end of 2012 at the latest. Non-centrally cleared contracts should be subject to higher capital requirements."[32] In addition, it was decided that OTC derivatives contracts should be reported to trade repositories. Opaqueness around bilateral net exposures of systemically important financial institutions (SIFIs) caused risk

---

* Valuable research assistance and input by Cosmina Amariei and Diego Valiante for this chapter are gratefully acknowledged.
[32] G-20, Leaders Statement, Pittsburgh Summit, p. 9.

aversion and froze the interbank market, with broader implications for credit markets at global level.

Together with the reinforcement of bank capital, mandatory central trading and clearing of standardised OTC derivatives are the most important shifts brought about by the financial crisis, but many uncertainties yet remain. The capacity of the industry's infrastructure to clear millions of transactions and to facilitate collateral and counterparty risk management (such as portfolio compression and reconciliation) in order to minimise adverse effects on credit availability is only part of the challenge. Another issue is the resilience of CCPs as mutual risk absorbers. In addition, centralised repositories for all OTC derivatives trades were established. The initiatives in the settlement arena, both at the Commission and at ECB level, were already on the agenda well before the financial crisis hit, but the resolve to pursue harmonised rules and a single settlement engine crystallised as a result.

This chapter analyses four components of the measures affecting securities and derivative markets: 1) the rules regarding central clearing of derivative financial instruments as contained in the European market infrastructure Regulation (EMIR) ; 2) the regulatory framework for and supervision of CCPs under the new EMIR legislation; 3) the authorisation requirements of trade repositories; and 4) the central securities depository (CSD) Regulation and the progress with the ECB's Target 2 Securities (T2S) project. The chapter concludes with an assessment of the new rules on financial infrastructures.

4.1 The anatomy of EMIR

CCPs play a key role in the financial system, but their function primarily affects a few players in the market. The OTC derivative market on both sides of the Atlantic has been so far dominated by nine players, which control more than 80% of the market (Valiante, 2010). The explicit and implicit costs for participating in CCPs and the impact on their profitability is a key factor for these players, as well as the related reduction in systemic risk. The question remains whether risk is better controlled when 'multilateralised' and internalised in CCPs, or whether we are creating even larger pools of risk.

For central clearing to occur, much depends on the eligibility of OTC derivatives, which amounts to about two-thirds of the market, and the governance and control of CCPs. Of the largest part of OTC derivative markets, the interest rates swap market, 86% has become clearable, and only a fraction remains non-clearable.[33] But offloading contracts that are clearable may leave bilateral derivative markets with 'tail-risk' exposures, which may importantly affect markets and increase risks to be taken up by financial institutions. Ultimately, the costs of bilateral trading of complex products that cannot be cleared on highly standardised platforms will inevitably increase.

Figure 3. Notional amounts outstanding, gross market value, gross credit exposure of OTC derivatives (€ trillion)

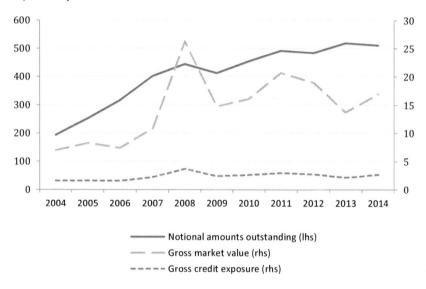

Notional amounts outstanding (lhs)
Gross market value (rhs)
Gross credit exposure (rhs)

Notes: The *notional amount outstanding* represents a market size indicator and is defined as the gross nominal or notional value of all deals concluded and not yet settled on the reporting date. The *gross market value* represents the cost of replacing all outstanding contracts at current market prices. Finally, *gross credit exposure* looks at the gross market values after legally enforceable bilateral netting but before collateral is taken out.

Data source: BIS (2014).

---

[33] According to Michael Davie of LCH Clearnet (2014).

The European market infrastructure Regulation (EMIR) remains in its final text very much at the level of principles in the prudential requirements for CCPs and the eligibility of derivatives for central clearing.[34] These were further substantiated in delegated acts, of which the European Commission has issued 17 different acts so far. The minimum requirements for CCPs and the rules governing TRs are already applicable, whereas the requirements for central clearing and the collateralisation for non-centrally cleared derivatives are still in the course of implementation. The first regulation on the classes of over-the-counter (OTC) derivatives to be subject to the clearing obligation was adopted by the Commission on 6 August 2015, foreseeing a gradual three-year implementation period.[35] But this is at least two years later than the similar rule under the US Dodd-Frank Bill, and already led to a shift in derivatives trading from the US to the EU (ISDA, 2014).

Non-financial corporations and pension funds (for a three-year transition period) are exempt from the scope of the regulation. The exemption for non-financial corporations was already on the agenda well before the text was formally proposed, and was maintained, albeit with the maintenance of a clearing threshold. The same applies in the US under Dodd-Frank, which came into effect in October 2013. The exemption for pension funds was a major success of lobbying with the European Parliament, but does not apply in the US.

The exemption from the scope of the regulation for non-financial corporations applies below a clearing threshold of €1 billion for credit and equity derivatives, and €3 billion for currency, interest rate, commodity and other OTC derivatives (Art. 10, EMIR; Art. 10, p. 82, ESMA, 2012). In addition, transactions that are considered positions that reduce risks directly related to the commercial or treasury-financing activities of the non-financial entity, the so-called 'hedging transactions' (Art. 10.3, EMIR), will not contribute to the clearing threshold. Following ESMA standards

---

[34] Regulation (EU) No 648/2012 of the European Parliament and of the Council of 4 July 2012 on OTC derivatives, central counterparties and trade repositories, OJ L 201 of 27.07.2012.

[35] Commission delegated regulation (EU) of 6.8.2015 supplementing Regulation (EU) No 648/2012 of the European Parliament and of the Council with regard to regulatory technical standards on the clearing obligation.

(Art. 9.1 (a)(b)(c), p. 82, ESMA, 2012; based on Art. 10.3, EMIR), 'hedging' may assume a broad meaning, i.e. all transactions that are done to indirectly or directly mitigate price risk, or are compliant with IFRS standards (Art. 3, Regulation no. 1606/2002).

The exemption from central clearing for pension schemes is less clear cut, as it is only applicable during a transition period of three years. The representatives of pension schemes successfully argued that the margin requirements of CCPs would reduce returns for future retirees. However, pension schemes will be subject to reporting obligations and bilateral collateralisation requirements. "The ultimate aim is, however, central clearing as soon as this is tenable" (Recital 15, EMIR). This derogation also applies to group insurance schemes, provided they are ring-fenced from other activities within the insurance group (Art. 2.10(c)).

Bilateral contracts that are not centrally cleared are subject to strict risk management procedures and operational requirements (such as collateralisation, portfolio reconciliation and affirmation/confirmation systems).[36] The value of outstanding contracts shall be marked-to-market on a daily basis, except if the market is inactive (a quoted price is not readily available or fair value estimates are too divergent) (Art. 15, p. 85, ESMA, 2012).

4.2 Authorisation and operational requirements for a CCP

EMIR follows a dual approach for the authorisation of CCPs. EU-based CCP's are authorised by the relevant authorities in their home country, in most cases the bank supervisors. Authorised third-country CCPs can be recognised to do business in the EU by ESMA, subject to an equivalence decision by the European Commission and an ESMA cooperation agreement with the respective home supervisory authority on exchange of information. Some 16 CCPs have been authorised from within the EU (ESMA, March 2015), while an equivalence decision was concluded with four countries in South East Asia: Australia, Hong Kong, Japan and Singapore. The equivalence with the US has been pending for some time.

---

[36] Another important service is compression, which allows netted positions to be further reduced (early termination) against each other at an agreed mark-to-market valuation of the contract (Art. 3 RM, ESMA, 2012).

Once the initial conditions are met, clearing houses can offer their services freely within the EU, after notifying the host-country authorities. Previously, further to MiFID (Arts 34 and 37 in MiFID II), investment firms could have access to host-country clearing and settlement services, but the latter could not provide their services freely across borders, which is what EMIR, and the CSD Regulation, now put in place.

The basic prudential and business conduct standards for CCPs today comprise:

1. an "adequate" capitalisation of at least €7.5 million, "proportional" to the risk taken by the CCP (Art. 16);[37]

2. exposure management, margining rules, a pre-funded default fund, the default waterfall or the financial safeguards available to a CCP to cover losses arising from a clearing member (CM) default, collateralisation and investment policy (Arts 40-47); and

3. governance and conduct requirements (segregated and portable individual client accounts, conflicts of interest rules, outsourcing policy, Arts 33-39).

These rules, and above all those under item (2), are key to the well-functioning of CCPs. They were further substantiated in technical standards, guidelines and recommendations that were issued by EBA and ESMA. Doubts, however, remain among specialists regarding the resilience of CCPs. Much depends upon the internal risk management methodologies of CCPs, whose operators call for greater transparency and disclosure of the results of the stress testing regime (see e.g. LCH Clearnet, 2014). The limited research on the subject demonstrates the heterogeneity of CCPs and of the members of CCPs, which should be a reason for concern on the part of policy-makers.

Regulatory capital is required to cover gross operational expenses for winding down and restructuring the CCP. On top of this, capital is needed to cover operational, legal, and non-covered

---

[37] It should be proportional to the "risk stemming from the activities of the CCP" (Recital 48 and Art. 16.2). This is a very open clause, which – for CCPs licensed as banks – could also create conflicts with current capital requirements (EBA will need to set regulatory technical standards for this). CCPs could also be subject to other capital requirements regulations.

credit, and counterparty and market risks. Calculations are set in the capital requirements Regulation (CRR), which comprise as well the exposures of banks to CCPs and their contributions to a default fund.

As a consequence of market infrastructure surveillance, access to central bank liquidity, and capital requirement regulation, CCPs fall under the supervision of three European authorities, ESMA, EBA, and the ECB, apart from the local one. The list of the national competent authorities, as published by ESMA, comprises central banks, FSAs, securities markets regulators and ministries of finance, which does not facilitate supervision of entities that are very international by nature. It is structured in 'colleges of supervisors', whose operation is set in Art. 18 of EMIR, and subject to implementing technical standards, under the coordination of ESMA.

The access of CCPs to central bank liquidity facilities, and the relationship with the location of CCPs, have been high on the agenda since CCPs were given a central role in the financial system. CCPs are critical infrastructures that may need a central bank backstop in case of trouble. But the policy line of EU central banks has not been univocal. Whereas the Bank of England (BoE) has openly raised this possibility, the ECB was more reluctant, and indicated that this cannot be a given. This divergence of views came to light in an EU Court case between the UK and the ECB on the location of CCPs, and whether they could be constrained by the currency area in which CCPs are operating.

The ECB had stated in its Eurosystem Oversight Policy Framework (July 2011): "as a matter of principle, infrastructures that settle euro-denominated payment transactions should settle these transactions in central bank money and be legally incorporated in the euro area with full managerial and operational control and responsibility over all core functions for processing euro denominated transactions, exercised from within the euro area." The location policy is applied to all CCPs that hold on average more than 5% of the aggregate daily net credit exposure of all CCPs for one of the main euro-denominated product categories. The UK challenged this on the grounds that the ECB lacked the powers to dictate such rules and that it violated the single market principle.

The location of a CCP relates to the situation in which a CCP fails and needs central bank liquidity support to keep the financial system function orderly. Who should be in charge in case of a liquidity crisis? The central bank where the CCP is headquartered with its main operations, or perhaps the central bank where the main financial entities of the CCP are based or possibly the central bank of the main currency cleared on the CCP? In effect, EMIR cannot force the ECB and its network (ESCB) to intervene, but Recitals 11 and 53 emphasise the ESCB's important role in the process of licensing, supervision and support of the clearing and settlement system. ESMA worked very closely with the ECB in drafting the EMIR regulatory and technical standards.[38]

On 4 March 2015, the Court of Justice of the European Union (CJEU) annulled the ECB's European Oversight Policy Framework and ruled that the ECB lacked the competence necessary to regulate the activity of securities clearing systems, as its competence is limited to payment systems alone by Art. 127(2) of the FEU Treaty.[39] But the Court case did not address the issue of the access to central bank facilities.

Besides the moral hazard created by including the ECB in the supervisory process of a CCP, it is unclear how, if a CCP fails, the potential intervention of a central bank would look. Would the ECB intervene to inject liquidity (capital or credit line) in a CCP even though its failure is caused by the counterparty default of a US legal entity for knock-on effects of badly managed activities run in the US (whether the clearing member is a subsidiary or branch)?

This situation could be highly controversial. Three steps are possible in this case: 1) the central bank where the CCP is operating can step in and directly inject liquidity in the CCP, disregarding the composition and nationality of its clearing members (location plays then a key role); 2) the central bank of the main currency traded on the CCP would inject liquidity directly in the CCP; or 3) MoUs

---

[38] It should be recalled that the discussions on this item between the ECB and CESR, the predecessor of ESMA, have a long history. They started in 2001 and broke down in 2005 for about three years until the EU finance ministers mandated both in the context of the financial crisis to resume their work, leading to the ECB-CESR recommendations of June 2009, see www.ecb.eu/paym/pol/secover/escbcesr/html/index.en.html.

[39] Judgment in Case T-496/11, March 2015.

among central banks can actually regulate a common intervention based on the percentage of the default fund held by clearing members operating in the central bank's jurisdiction or under its supervision. For instance, if US clearing members' subsidiaries hold only 10% of the default fund, in case of liquidity problems, the Fed would only inject liquidity through a swap line for 10% of the total amount requested. The announcement made by the Bank of England and the ECB on 29 March 2015, as further to the Court judgement, indicated that third step would be followed: "The ECB and the BoE are today extending the scope of the standing swap line in order, should it be necessary and without pre-committing to the provision of liquidity, to facilitate the provision of multi-currency liquidity support by both central banks to CCPs established in the UK and euro area respectively."[40]

In the US, the Financial Services Oversight Council (FSOC) is authorised under Title VIII, section 131, of the Dodd-Frank Act to designate a financial market utility (FMU) as 'systemically important' in cases where a failure of or a disruption to the functioning of an FMU could create, or increase, the risk of significant liquidity or credit problems spreading among financial institutions or markets and thereby threaten the stability of the US financial system. Currently designated FMUs, including five clearing entities[41] supervised by the Board of the FSOC, the CFTC (Commodity Futures Trading Commission) or the SEC, are subject to heightened prudential and supervisory provisions.

Defining an appropriate recovery and resolution framework for CCPs is most probably the next regulatory challenge for both EU and US regulators. There are many things to be clarified, most notably when recovery and resolution should be triggered, the tools to be used in each situation, and the nature of the resolution authority.

---

[40] www.ecb.europa.eu/press/pr/date/2015/html/pr150329.en.html.

[41] The Clearing House Payments Company, L.L.C., on the basis of its role as operator of the Clearing House Interbank Payments System - (Board); Fixed Income Clearing Corporation - (SEC); ICE Clear Credit L.L.C. - (CFTC); National Securities Clearing Corporation - (SEC); and the Options Clearing Corporation - (SEC).

As a follow-up to the publication of the "Principles for financial market infrastructures" (April, 2012) and "Principles for financial market infrastructures: disclosure framework and assessment methodology" (December, 2012) CPMI and IOSCO published in October 2014 a report on "Recovery of financial market infrastructures"[42] and in February 2015 the "Public quantitative disclosure standards for central counterparties".[43] Also, the FSB published a report on the "Key Attributes of Effective Resolution Regimes for Financial Institutions", which includes an annex dedicated to resolution regimes for FMIs.[44] These reports and principles are important milestones for all 28 jurisdictions. The European Commission is expected to publish a legislative proposal in 2015 on resolution and recovery of financial market infrastructures such as CCPs.

For cash securities, CCPs may enter into interoperability arrangements provided certain criteria are met (Arts 51-53). These include interoperability with other CCPs and non-discriminatory data access to trading venues and settlement systems (Art. 51.2). ESMA had to report by end-2014 on the appropriateness of the extension of these interoperability arrangements to non-cash securities. In any case, counterparties can voluntarily enter into a bilateral interoperability agreement for non-cash securities, to be agreed by the authorities.

The interoperability agreements are approved by national authorities, but ultimately ESMA can only issue a non-binding opinion (reconsidering clause) in case disagreement persists among the financial authority granting/denying approval and the financial authority where the CCP is located (Art. 54.3). This lack of power may affect the implementation of this requirement if the dispute among national authorities is not solved by ESMA's moral suasion, especially if ESMA perceives that the national authority has not correctly interpreted the requirements set by the regulation.

---

[42] CPMI-IOSCO Report, October 2014 (www.bis.org/cpmi/publ/d121.pdf).

[43] CPMI-IOSCO Principles, February 2015
(www.bis.org/cpmi/publ/d125.pdf).

[44] FSB Report, October 2014 (www.financialstabilityboard.org/wp-content/uploads/r_141015.pdf).

Arts 7 and 8, and Recital 34 of EMIR set a 'reverse' open access principle, also included in the markets in financial instruments Regulation (MiFIR, Arts 28 and 29), but applicable to all financial instruments.[45] As a result, a competing CCP would get access to data feeds from the incumbent trading venue to offer clearing services in competition, and vice versa. The incumbent CCP would need to accept to clear transactions executed in different trading venues, so as to allow competing trading venues to compete with the incumbent trading platform on reasonable terms. Access to these services should be non-discriminatory, and it should not create the need for interoperability or liquidity fragmentation.[46] In case either of these two conditions cannot be met, the incumbent can deny access. Even if the 'liquidity fragmentation' condition has been clearly defined by ESMA, requirements to establish when open access may need interoperability are unclear, which may leave space for market players to claim an arbitrary need to be interoperable in order to deny access (whether or not this is true).

In addition, it is difficult to imagine CCPs competing without interoperability agreements in place, as this would imply sealing pools of collateral in vertical infrastructures and ultimately increasing costs. The risk of locking the system into a collection of sealed pools of collateral that are unable to talk to each other may drastically reduce the efficiency (and ultimately the stability) of the financial system. However, interoperability for derivatives is difficult to achieve because of the different nature and characteristics of these transactions, e.g. correlation among products. Against this background, technologies in this area are progressing quickly and competition among CCPs will certainly escalate in the near future around the provision of services that can improve the management of collateral and generate important savings for end users, ultimately leading to a more interoperable environment.

---

[45] The current version of the text discussed within the European Parliament.

[46] Following ESMA (Art. 8, p. 81, ESMA, 2012), there is no "liquidity fragmentation" if there is at least one CCP in common (after the competing CCP is allowed to enter) and there are already clearing arrangements established by the CCP.

4.3   Trade repositories

Trade repositories centrally collect and maintain the records of any derivative contract that has been concluded and any modification or termination of the contract. All derivative contracts must be reported to a trade repository within one business day of execution (T+1). This applies to both cleared and non-cleared trades, both listed and OTC derivatives, swaps outstanding and pre-enacted. This report must include the parties to and main characteristics of the contract.

Until the eve of the crisis, limited information was available on the OTC derivatives contracts outstanding, and for those existing, no harmonised international standards existed. Opaqueness in derivative markets caused disruptive adverse selection effects in the interbank market, following Lehman Brothers' bankruptcy. Only one trade repository, the US DTCC, had been in existence since before the financial crisis, covering only credit derivatives. However, several new initiatives – such as Regis-TR (joint initiative of Iberclear and Clearstream) – have been launched in the meantime and recently started operations.

Trade repositories are authorised by ESMA, and its doing so becomes, in addition to authorising rating agencies, the second specific and unique supervisory task that it will perform. In return for doing so, ESMA charges fees to the repositories, which should fully cover its expenses. ESMA may delegate supervisory tasks to member state authorities. Six trade repositories were formally recognised by ESMA in early 2015. Trade repositories from third countries may also be recognised, as soon as an equivalence agreement with the country in question has been concluded (Art. 75). As for other EU directives, the use of an 'equivalence' regime raises questions about the criteria used to determine equivalence. Too strict an equivalence regime would ring-fence EU markets and affect linkages with non-EU counterparties, while too lax an equivalence regime would create space for regulatory arbitrage.

To ensure a proper supervisory framework works, ESMA has the powers to undertake general investigations, do on-site inspections of and eventually impose fines upon trade repositories. This is, in a European context, a fairly new concept, although it also appears already in the Credit Rating Agencies Regulation (see

Chapter 2). Data collected by trade repositories should be made available to the relevant European and national supervisory authorities.

Notwithstanding the formal obligation to report, the market for trade repositories will remain small and highly concentrated. This market is, like the market for market data, global, with high scale economies and where only few players may emerge. Trade repositories should be interconnected and exchange information, with regulators defining mandatory formats for them to be capable of communicating with each other (Benito, 2012). It remains to be seen whether this will happen, as this has been an issue in the market data world as well for a long time, without much progress. Commercial interests in setting joint standards and exchange information may be minimal, which is fully recognised in the EMIR text (Recital 42). As a result, trade repositories should provide information on non-discriminatory terms, while regulation should clearly define how much information they can retain for commercial purposes (analytical data services) and how much should be disclosed to the market. The presence of multiple trade repositories, adopting the same standards and sharing information in order to reconcile a global picture of the market, can promote further competition among them in the provision of additional services to support middle office operations, e.g. confirmation, and collateral services, e.g. compression and real-time risk management, or just reporting services to regulators. In addition, trade repositories could also collect data in other less transparent areas, such as securities lending and repo operations, where transparency today is based on surveys and voluntary bilateral agreements between dealers and data vendors.

4.4 The CSD Regulation and T2S

After clearing with EMIR, the single license facilities will also apply to central securities depositories (CSDs), which hitherto had only been subject to a self-regulatory code. While the 2006 Code made some progress in the area of price transparency, hard-core issues such as interoperability and service unbundling did not advance, as too much was at stake for the operators. The CSD Regulation defines settlement, the settlement cycle (T+2) and settlement discipline, with penalties for settlement failures. It requires transparent access criteria, price and fee transparency, and interoperability between CSDs and with other infrastructures, such as CCPs (chapter IV). An 'equivalence' regime for recognition to provide services in the European Union, as with EMIR, applies to third-country CSDs (Art. 25).

The CSD Regulation sets for the first time harmonised prudential rules for CSDs in the EU. Although general global standards have existed since 2002, and were updated by the CPSS-IOSCO in the principles for financial market infrastructures (April 2012), the EU had left this until recently to the member states, which has hampered cross-border provision of settlement services in the EU. The regulation sets harmonised organisational requirements, conduct of business rules, rules for other CSD services, prudential standards and requirements for links with other CSDs. Authorisation is in the hands of the member states, with ESMA in charge of maintaining a CSD register. The regulation also establishes that member states should provide for a harmonised minimum level of administrative sanctions (including authorisation withdrawals) to be applied in case of breaches of the regulation to legal and natural persons (Art. 65).[47] Considering Banking Union and Target 2 Securities (T2S), the final settlement engine of the ECB, authorisation of and sanctions against CSDs would fit more logically with the ECB, but this seemed a bridge too far.

In addition to specific operational requirements such as daily reconciliation of the number of securities with the accounts, CSDs should segregate accounts of each participant and enable participants to segregate clients' individual accounts (Art. 38). Provision of cash settlement services in commercial bank money must be done though a separate credit institution or can be done through its own accounts (Art. 40). The combination of both functions in a CSD had given rise to discussions on the draft regulation, and resulted in a separate article setting special conditions for authorisation (Art. 54). It requires CSDs in both cases to have a banking licence in line with CRD IV in case it falls within the same legal entity or when it is a separate legal entity, and can be

---

[47] Administrative fines can go up to 10% of total turnover of a legal entity or to 10% of total income of a natural person or to €5 million. The combined use of 10% threshold in some countries and fixed €5 million threshold may still keep substantial divergences among EU countries.

subject to capital surcharges and additional prudential requirements. Authorities are allowed to designate more than one credit institution for cash-settlement services in case the concentration of risks is too high (Art. 54.6). Fears that securities accounts would be misused to support banking activities emerged following cases in which clients lost assets due to banking activities being conducted by the same entity, such as securities lending. Moving these services under a different legal entity provides a clear separation between pure settlement services and banking activities. At the same time, in combination with open-access rules, this may increase competition with other entities providing value added services across markets and CSDs.

As CSDs will have to look downstream to expand their services with the arrival of T2S, they will come into even more direct competition with custodian banks, as well as with firms providing middle office services. In this context, the current phrasing of the provision regarding banking services may cause uncertainty for CSDs, at least in the short term, on the costs and future of their vertically integrated business model. The Commission may argue that this is only a legal cost, but besides additional administrative and regulatory costs, i.e. separate capital requirement, there is an issue of economies of scale and scope that might be lost by splitting activities across several entities. The question arises whether similar rules will *ceteris paribus* apply to custodian banks providing other banking type ancillary services.

As regards T2S, all eurozone CSDs and several non-eurozone CSDs had signed up to T2S, including the Swiss CSD SIX, allowing the ECB to have a moderately favourable business case on which to proceed.[48] According to the 2008 impact assessment, settlement costs could decline by about 30% if all Eurozone countries join (see Lannoo & Valiante, 2009). This would further decline with non-Eurozone countries signing up, such as the Nordic countries, which are part of the Euroclear group. The Bank of England has, however, indicated that it will not participate in the platform for sterling-denominated settlements.

The framework agreement for those CSDs joining T2S, published in October 2011, is over 700 pages, containing 54 articles

---

[48] See ECB press release, 3 July 2012.

divided over seven chapters. It contains amongst other things the pricing for the settlement services of T2S, which has constantly increased after the first estimates, reducing the original business case made by the ECB, i.e. an important reduction in settlement costs. The prices are expected to vary between €0.40 and €0.60, depending on the components of the service, which are on the higher end of the 2008 ECB business case (in scenario 1, all Eurozone countries participating). Additionally, as we pointed out before (Lannoo & Valiante, 2009), T2S will also force efficient business models to charge more than what they actually charge today as they have 'agreed' to migrate to the T2S infrastructure.

Despite uncertainty around costs and who ultimately bears the operational risks, the EU institution-driven settlement platform is trying to succeed where market-driven solutions were not capable of progressing at the same pace, due to conflicting commercial interests, i.e. the creation of a harmonised framework for securities (and cash, with Target 2) settlement infrastructure. As a result of this initiative, competition among CSDs and providers of related services, e.g. global custodians, will become harsher on value added services and potentially on middle office services too, while small national players will be gradually pushed out of the market.

4.5   The EMIR revolution?

The new rules, as always, provide costs and benefits for the market. As with MiFID after the 2004 adoption, much debate was over costs, but the dynamic effects of the new rules in technological investment to compete in the new market environment are often underestimated. For end users, whether financial or non-financial institutions, the costs of collateral will certainly increase, at least in the short term.

At the end of 2013, according to ISDA (2014a), over 90% of bilateral OTC transactions were subject to collateral agreements with cash and government securities accounting for roughly 90% of the $3.2 trillion estimated amount of collateral in circulation. Roughly $100 trillion of OTC derivatives contracts (as notional value) do not have any collateral agreement in place, but collateralisation is growing at a quick pace. The reported collateral received and delivered against $407 trillion in notional amounts outstanding of centrally cleared OTC derivative transactions totalled roughly $295 trillion.

At end of 2013, the estimated uncollateralised exposure amounted to $1.45 trillion (see Figure 4), representing 47.72% of the gross credit exposure. As a result of current reforms and technological developments, the uncollateralised exposure has been constantly going down as the market developed, even before the crisis and despite the growth of volumes in the market. After the initial spike in uncollateralised exposure during the worst moment of the financial crisis, the combination of risk aversion in 2008-09 and market reforms in the last couple of years have pushed additional collateralisation into the system. These results are in line with a number of studies that looked at the expected increase in collateralisation as part of the envisaged OTC derivative markets reforms. According to a report prepared by the Macroeconomic Assessment Group on Derivatives (MAGD, 2013), these reforms will result in the total amount of collateral used to back trades rising to between €1.1 trillion and €1.8 trillion, with a central estimate of €1.3 trillion. Tabb Group estimated the need for collateral to be around $2 trillion. The European Commission (2010) estimated this exposure roughly to $1.4 trillion.

*Figure 4. Estimation of the uncollateralised exposure**

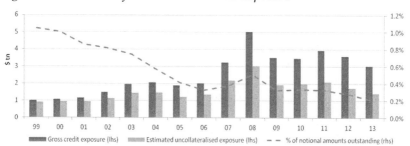

* Collateralisation further reduces gross credit exposure. In order to estimate the level of under-collateralisation, 50% of the collateral in circulation (as estimated in the ISDA Margin Surveys) is subtracted from the gross credit exposure (as reported in the BIS semi-annual surveys).

Source: Authors' own configuration based on BIS and ISDA data.

Essential to this process is the creation of a modern and flexible infrastructure that optimises the use of collateral and allows offering diversified services for end users. This situation, on the one side, creates a lot of opportunities for the industry to develop, through new technologies, competitive services such as real-time risk management services, or cross-asset classes clearing. On the other side, it clashes with commercial interests that impede initiatives to make collateral pools more fungible to promote interoperable clearing platforms with other CCPs (mainly through cross-margining agreements).

By setting risk management procedures among CCPs and instituting strict day-to-day supervision under the ESMA-ECB umbrella, an interoperable environment would certainly deliver better collateral management and huge savings for end users, a key element for the creation of a truly pan-European infrastructure. EMIR is very timid in this area and it sees interoperability as a threat to the stability of the CCP (interoperability will only be limited to 'cash securities'). However, the lack of fungible collateral pools would itself be a threat to the efficiency of the market as it could create costly sealed CCP operations, which would increase the need for collateral. In effect, two CCPs at the two sides of the same transaction may ask for the same amount of collateral, which will represent a costly duplication.

In an interoperable framework, once risk management procedures are fixed and well-supervised, competition among CCPs would move to value added services linked to collateral management. In any case, EMIR will lead to investment in new clearing technologies, as the current clearing technology is neither scalable nor flexible enough to handle the changes that are coming (Tabb Group, 2011). As a result of better technology, moving potentially to almost real-time clearing will increase transaction volumes and liquidity, and so will the pie for market participants that enter into the arena. Shortening settlement cycles will also free more capital, which can be redeployed to improve market efficiency.

In addition to the implications for clearing and CCP business, costs of membership in and reporting to trade repositories should also be considered. EMIR, in effect, creates huge opportunities for trade repositories, too, and the expected volume increase in traded and cleared derivatives will further stimulate their growth. Existing organisations in clearing, trading and data reporting may benefit from this change, provided they have made the necessary adaptations.

For this to happen, competition between CCPs will need to be strengthened, and interoperability enforced in the exchange-traded derivatives (ETD) space. Synergies with ETD may expand oligopolistic settings in adjacent markets ('cross-subsidisation'), such as the unlisted OTC derivatives clearing space. Access to the respective CCPs by competing trading venues and by competing CCPs to the incumbent trading venue (reverse open access) is constrained because of closed vertical silos, i.e. there is no direct access to the data feed of the incumbent trading venue by competing CCPs and no possibility by competing trading venues to share a data feed with the incumbent CCP. This lack of competition may further limit growth and innovation in the EU's derivative markets.

As compared to the US, where anecdotal evidence suggests that the market grew by 35% in the post-crisis period, the EU's exchange traded derivative market was rather stagnant. This is also why the European Commission prohibited the merger between the NYSE and D-Börse, which would have "created a quasi-monopoly in a number of asset classes, leading to significant harm to derivatives users and the European economy as a whole. With no effective competitive constraint left in the market, the benefits of price competition would be taken away from customers. There would also be less innovation in an area where a competitive market is vital for both SMEs and larger firms."[49] The implementation of EMIR should bring more competition to these markets, while allowing European competition policy authorities to better monitor markets.

---

[49] The European Commission blocked the proposed merger between Deutsche Börse and NYSE Euronext after the companies' refusal to apply tough conditions and sell the part of their business that was creating strong concentration, see press release, 1 February 2012 (http://europa.eu/rapid/press-release_IP-12-94_en.htm?locale=en).

4.6 Conclusions

With a delay of more than 10 years, the EU is finally putting a regulatory framework in place for the post-trade financial market infrastructure. As a result of the financial crisis, this regulatory framework is following two important trends. On the one side, there is the general mandate given by the G-20 to regulators to strengthen financial stability, mainly through transparency and mandatory use of highly standardised infrastructures for clearing OTC derivatives transactions. On the other side, since the launch of the Financial Services Action Plan in 1999, Europe has been trying to build a pan-European infrastructure framework leveraging on healthy competition among national incumbent settlement infrastructures and new pan-European competitors.

Europe should continue to work to ensure stability without compromising the high-level goal of greater integration through competition at pan-European level, and a common market architecture with minimum standards through more effective ongoing supervision and enforcement. Any attempt by market operators to impede competition along the long value chain of financial market infrastructure on unfounded grounds should be considered an attack on the single market. However, it cannot be denied either that profitability will go down drastically for market infrastructures. Due to fiercer competition, revenues may go down even further, so – in order to remain commercially viable – they need to integrate their businesses vertically (greater consolidation among trading, clearing and settlement providers is already part of the process) and horizontally to create economies of scale (size) and scope (services).

EMIR, in particular on the mandatory clearing side, has spurred a sea change, since a new market emerged for central clearing of hitherto bilaterally traded derivative contracts. Huge investments have been made and are still to come in clearing technology and value added services, which will bring important changes in the coming years. Existing CCPs will see huge opportunities for growth, and new ones can be expected to emerge. On the settlement side, free competition between CSDs may lead to further concentration and horizontal consolidation within the sector, as this is a scale business *par excellence*, but also to greater competition with specialised banks for the expansion of territory.

With growing concentration in the clearing and settlement sector, the task for macro and prudential supervisors will not become easier. However, as long as the regulatory and supervisory frameworks ensure that these integrated infrastructures are sufficiently interoperable, i.e. open at each key juncture of their value chain (trading, clearing and settlement), the process of 'pan-Europeanisation' of the market infrastructure will continue and be beneficial for financial integration. Locking collateral and customers in vertical and non-interoperable market infrastructures may also have spillover effects on trading flows, by distorting flows from non-vertically integrated infrastructures. In the short term, this may generate predatory practices by vertically integrated and non-interoperable market infrastructures to push infrastructures that are unable to ring-fence collateral pools with post-trading operations out of the market. This may drive further consolidation but with limited benefits in terms of efficiency as these pools of collateral will be unable (and unwilling) to interact.

A problem on the supervisory side is the multiplicity of actors, with three different bodies in charge at European level alone: the ECB (and other central banks), ESMA and EBA, and with licensing and supervision still in the hands of local authorities, contrary to what was initially envisaged. With Banking Union, a more streamlined structure will be necessary, given also that it concerns only a few players, and of systemic importance. In addition, close cooperation between the two major European supervisors, the ECB and the Bank of England, will be required, in the form of a MoU to structure control, as was done for CCPs after the EU Court decision on the location of CCPs.

Finally, more light should be shed on the implications of market infrastructure regulation on the availability of collateral (total volumes), and in particular on the possibility for this collateral and assets, if segregated in individual client accounts by CCPs and for settlement and custody by CSDs, to be reused for other purposes ('re-hypothecation') or to limit its reuse by the infrastructure/intermediary. Securities lending and repo markets in Europe have topped out, following our prudent estimate, at more than €6 trillion.[50] In the end, much will also depend on how each CCP will draft the "right of use" policy of the collateral, in line with the guidelines set by Art. 47 on the investment policy of a CCP (and Art. 52.1 on risk management procedures with interoperability agreements). The entire financial system depends on the integrity and turnover of collateral channels (Sissoko, 2011; Singh & Stella, 2012), on which the market has leveraged and grown so rapidly in the last decade. Any change that generates indirect effects on the architecture of the financial system should be subject to thorough investigation and a testing period to assess potential unintended effects and new sources of systemic risk.

References

Amariei, C. and D. Valiante (2014), "The OTC derivatives markets after financial reforms", ECMI Policy Brief, European Capital Markets Institute, Brussels, May.

Armakolaa, Angela and Jean-Paul Laurent (2015) "CCP resilience and clearing membership, July, mimeo.

Bank of England (2012), "Financial Stability Report", June.

Benito, J. (2012), "The role of market infrastructures in OTC derivative markets", *Journal of Securities Operations & Custody*, Vol. 4, No. 4.

BIS (2014), Semi-annual OTC derivatives statistics, Basel, November and May.

CPSS-IOSCO and BIS (2012), "Principles for financial market infrastructures", April (www.bis.org/publ/cpss101a.pdf).

Deutsche Bank (2012), "Global Derivatives Reform Progress to Date", June.

European Banking Authority (2012), Draft Regulatory Technical Standards on capital requirements for CCPs, (www.eba.europa.eu/cebs/media/Publications/standards/EB A-DraftRTS-2012-01--Draft-RTS-on-capital-requirements-for-CCPs---WITH-CORRECTED-TYPOS.pdf).

European Council and the European Parliament (2012), EU Regulation n. 648/2012 on OTC derivatives, central counterparties and trade repositories (EMIR), 4 July.

---

[50] Authors' estimates based on data from International Securities Lending Association and International Capital Markets Association.

European Commission (2010), Impact Assessment on EMIR, SEC(2010) 1058/2 (http://ec.europa.eu/internal_market/financial-markets/docs/derivatives/20100915_impact_assessment_en.pdf).

European Commission (2012), Proposal for a Regulation on improving securities settlement in the European Union and on central securities depositories (CSDs) and amending Directive 98/26/EC (http://ec.europa.eu/internal_market/financial-markets/central_securities_depositories_en.htm#proposal).

European Securities and Markets Authority (2012), "Final Report on EMIR Draft Technical Standards", ESMA/2012/600, 27 September.

ISDA (2014), "Cross-Border Fragmentation of Global OTC Derivatives: An Empirical Analysis", Research Note, January.

ISDA (2014a), "Margin Survey" (www2.isda.org/functional-areas/research/surveys/margin-surveys/).

Lannoo, K. and D. Valiante (2009), "Integrating Europe's Back Office: 10 years of turning in circles", ECMI Policy Brief No. 13, European Capital Markets Institute, Brussels, June.

LCH Clearnet (2014), "CCP risk management, recovery & resolution", An LCH Clearnet White Paper, November.

MAGD (2013), "Macroeconomic impact assessment of OTC derivatives regulatory reforms", September.

Singh, M. (2011), "Velocity of pledged collateral", IMF Working Paper, International Monetary Fund, Washington, D.C., November (www.imf.org/external/pubs/ft/wp/2011/wp11256.pdf).

Singh, M. and P. Stella (2012), "Money and Collateral", IMF Working Paper No. 12/95, International Monetary Fund, Washington, D.C.

Sissoko, C. (2011), "The legal foundations of financial collapse" (http://papers.ssrn.com/sol3/papers.cfm?abstract_id=1525120)

Tabb Group (2011), "OTC Derivatives Clearing Technology: Bringing the Back Office to the Forefront", September.

Valiante, D. (2010), "Shaping Reforms and Business Models for the OTC Derivatives Market: Quo vadis?", ECMI Research Report No. 5, European Capital Markets Institute, Brussels, April.

5. NEW CAPITAL REQUIREMENTS: BASEL III IMPLEMENTATION IN EU LAW*

The new bank capital requirements serve as the centrepiece of the post-crisis regulatory set-up, at global as well as EU level, but they are also the most complex part of it – and possibly excessively so. The EU capital rules build on what has been designed by an international committee, the Basel Committee, since the late 1980s, and have been adapted to the European circumstances. But compared to earlier versions, CRR/CRD IV contains real harmonisation, compared to previous attempts which left far too much leeway to the member states and to the banks. The loopholes in Basel II were called "one of the major factors of the crisis" by Mario Draghi, in his former capacity as Chairman of the Financial Stability Board.[51]

During the financial crisis, the losses of many banks wiped out their total capital base, even though the latter had been above the amount required by regulation. Figure 5 shows the annual returns as a share of risk-weighted assets for the top percentiles of the largest European banks during the crisis years, also subdivided according to business model. In more than one in 100 bank-year observations, the single-year losses were for all banks more than the total capital the banks were required to hold. In particular, the losses of the top percentiles of the banks focusing on retail activities and the banks conducting more investment activities were substantial.

---

* This chapter was drafted with the useful help of Willem Pieter De Groen.

[51] In his remarks at the Conference on Financial Integration and Stability, organised by the European Commission and the ECB, Brussels, 2 May 2011 (http://ec.europa.eu/internal_market/economic_analysis/conference201105 02_en.htm).

Figure 5. Return on risk-weighted assets (top percentiles)

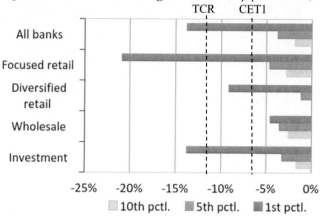

Note: This figure depicts the return on risk-weighted assets (RoRWA) of the top percentiles (1st, 5th, and 10th) for the 147 largest and most systemic banks in the EU and Norway for the period 2006-13. The dotted lines show the minimum regulatory requirements under CRD IV, common equity Tier 1 (CET1) requirement of 4.5% and total capital ratio (TCR) requirement of 8% respectively.

Source: Ayadi & De Groen (2014).

Basel III should reduce the likelihood of a bank default, while the resolution mechanisms should reduce the costs to taxpayers of a bank default. Basel III is a regime change as compared to Basel II, as it tightens the definition of capital and requires capital buffers and add-ons for large systemically important banks, and macro-prudential buffers. Basel III also not only targets solvency, but also liquidity. But one important part was not modified, the risk-weighting of assets, and the related internal models to calculate risk weights, meaning that an important advantage remains for large banks. Another change compared to the previous translation of the Basel agreements in EU legislation is in the method of harmonisation. Most of the EU rules are now packed in a directly applicable regulation (CRR), rather than in a directive (CRD IV), which is transposed in national law. In response to the financial crisis, member states agreed on a 'single rulebook', meaning that exactly the same rules should apply all across the EU, and that loopholes as a result of differences in interpretation should be banned. This has added an additional level of complexity in the technical standard setting, which is still an ongoing process.

The EU is the only jurisdiction fully 'codifying' Basel III for application and implementation in the national law of 31 states, whose financial systems collectively represent over 40% of global banking assets. Other jurisdictions leave this responsibility mostly to the discretion of national supervisory authorities. EU-licensed banks may thus feel more constrained than their counterparties in third countries.

This chapter starts with an explanation of the structure of CRR/CRD IV, followed by the focal elements: capital requirements, liquidity rules and reporting requirements.

5.1 Structure of CRR and CRD IV

CRR/CRD IV is hugely complex, composed of a Regulation containing 521 articles and four annexes and a Directive consisting of 165 articles and one annex. Its size alone makes it a monster. The Regulation addresses elements that must be harmonised at EU level, whereas the Directive deals with elements, including capital buffers, on which member states can have leeway (see Table 4). Both make ample references to secondary law, which have kept the EBA busy since the adoption of both measures in 2013.

Table 4. Comparison of CRR/CRD IV

CRR (R=Regulation)	CRD (D=Directive)
Definitions	Authorisation
Scope	Competences of supervisors
Definition of capital	Sanctions
Solvency requirements	Governance
Large exposures	Remuneration
Retention requirements	Consolidation supervision
Liquidity coverage ratio	Pillar II
Leverage ratio	Capital buffer provisions
Disclosure ('Pillar III')	
Transitional arrangements	

Source: DNB (2013).

The Regulation covers those prudential requirements for banks that need to be uniform across the EU to ensure a level playing field. CRR Recital 9 reads: "In order to avoid market distortions and regulatory arbitrage, prudential minimum requirements should therefore ensure maximum harmonisation", meaning that the minimum requirements shall be absolutely the same across member states. However, this does not stop individual institutions from having a higher level of own funds (Art. 3). The CRR sets the definition and composition of Common Equity Tier 1, Tier 1 and total capital, the leverage ratio and the capital requirements for credit risk under the different approaches. The Regulation further describes the standardised and internal ratings-based approach, with the risk-weightings according to external credit ratings or internal assessments, and the definitions of and exceptions to large exposures and the liquidity coverage ratio, and the disclosure of all this to the public.

The Directive addresses authorisation and the powers of home- and host-country authorities, governance requirements for banks and the thorny issue of remuneration, supervisory powers and review, consolidation, initial capital of banks and investment firms, capital buffers, including the capital conservation buffer, the institutions-specific countercyclical buffer, the globally systemically important institution buffer (G-SII), the other systemically important institution buffer (O-SII) and the systemic risk (or macro-prudential) buffer. Hence whereas the definition of capital is part of the regulation, the levels of capital are part of the directive. Member states can therefore decide to set higher capital requirements.

The Regulation and Directive delegate many tasks to the standard setters, to be confirmed by the European Commission in secondary legislation. CRR and CRD IV are complemented by no fewer than 49 Regulatory Technical Standards (RTS) and 26 Implementing Technical Standards (ITS), issued in 2013-15.

5.2 Capital

CRD IV is a radical change as compared to CRD I, not only in the level of capital, but also in its definition. What has not changed is the denominator, as the assets remain risk-weighted, with no or limited risk weights for crucial asset classes. A leverage ratio remains optional for the time being.

THE GREAT FINANCIAL PLUMBING | 89

Table 5. CRR/CRD IV capital and liquidity ratios

Ratios	(Minimum) Rate	Imple-mented	Calibration
Capital ratios			
Leverage ratio	3%	2018	Tier 1 capital/ Total exposure (On- and off-balance sheet assets)
Risk-adjusted capital ratios			
Common Equity Tier 1 capital (CET1)) ratio	4.5%	2018	CET1/ Risk-weighted exposure
Tier 1 capital ratio	6%	2018	Tier 1 capital (CET1 + Additional Tier 1 capital)/Risk-weighted exposure
Total capital ratio	8%	2018	Own funds (Tier 1 + Tier 2)/ Risk-weighted exposure
Capital buffers (1 to 3 are cumulative)			
Capital conservation buffer	2.5%	2019	Additional CET1 ratio
Countercyclical capital buffer	0-2.5%	2019	Additional CET1 ratio
G-SII and O-SII capital buffer	0-2-3.5%	2016	Additional CET1 ratio
Systemic risk buffer	0-3-5%	2015	Additional CET1 times exposure to which risk buffer applies
Liquidity ratios			
Liquidity coverage ratio (LCR)	100%	2018	High quality liquid assets/ Net liquidity outflows in 30-dayperiod
Net stable funding ratio (NSFR)	100%	2018	Available stable funding / Required stable funding

Although the basic minimum remains the same as in CRD I – 8% of Tier 1 and 2 – the definition of capital was tightened, and countercyclical and several other buffers were added, most importantly for large banks (G-SII and O-SII). This means that as a result of the bank or country specific capital requirement, the requirement could easily be double the 8%. Table 5 provides a complete overview of the capital and liquidity ratios that have been included in the EU implementation of Basel III. The Common Equity Tier 1 capital (CET1) is the purest form of capital (retained earnings and capital stock). The required level of CET1 increased from 2% under CRD I to 4.5% under CRD IV. Together with the additional Tier 1 capital, e.g. convertible capital instruments, CET1 forms the total going concern capital. The Tier 1 requirement has been increased, too, from 4% under CRD I to 6% under CRD IV.

In addition to going concern capital, the total regulatory capital ratio contains gone concern capital, i.e. Tier 2 capital. Whereas the definition of capital was tightened, the basic minimum of the total capital ratio remains the same at 8%. Countercyclical and several other buffers were added, most importantly for large banks (G-SIIs and O-SIIs). The buffers, which are mostly cumulative, are:

- **Capital conservation buffer**: Member states shall require institutions to maintain an additional capital conservation buffer of CET1) capital equal to 2.5% of their total risk exposure. Small and medium-sized investment firms may be exempted, but the Commission, EBA and European Systemic Risk Board (ESRB) need to be notified (CRD IV, Art. 129).

- **Countercyclical capital buffer**: Member states shall require institutions to maintain an additional countercyclical buffer of CET1 capital equal to up to 2.5% of their total risk exposure. Small and medium-sized investment firms may be exempted, but the Commission, EBA and ESRB need to be notified (CRD IV, Arts 130 and 136).

- **Systemically important institutions buffer**

  o **G-SII buffer**: Member states can require global systemically important institutions (G-SII) to maintain an additional capital buffer of CET1 capital equal to up to 3.5 % of their total risk exposure (from 1% for the lowest sub-category to 3.5% for the highest) (CRD IV, Art. 131). The G-SII identification is aligned with the

Financial Stability Board (FSB) framework for global systemically important banks (G-SIBs).

   o   **O-SII buffer**: Member states can require other systemically important institutions (O-SII) to maintain an additional capital buffer of CET1 capital equal to up to 2% of their total risk exposure. The Commission, the ESRB and EBA need to be notified about the buffer (CRD IV, Art. 131). The identification of G-SIIs and O-SIIs will be reviewed annually. In case of overlaps between the two SII categories, the higher level will apply.

- **Systemic risk buffer**: Member states can require institutions to maintain an additional capital buffer of CET1) capital equal to up to 5% of their total risk exposure (CRD IV, Art. 132). The risk buffer can apply to all exposures as well as to specific exposures. The Commission, the ESRB and EBA need to be notified about the buffer. For buffers in excess of 3%, the opinion of the Commission is required, taking into account the advice of the ESRB and EBA. When in agreement, the EU Commission shall then adopt an implementing act authorising the buffer (CRD IV, Art. 133, 12-15). When an institution is subject to both SII and systemic risk buffers, in principle the higher applies. Only when the systemic risk buffer for macro-prudential risks does not apply to exposures outside the member state is it cumulative to the SII buffers.

The capital conservation, countercyclical and G-SII buffers are similar to what is contained in the Basel III Accord; the O-SII and systemic risk buffers only apply in the EU. In addition, member states can also adopt macro-prudential measures, which can include the level of own fund requirements or a systemic risk buffer, but also other elements, such as changes in the risk weights and exposure limits (CRR, Art. 458). Such measures can only be adopted if not rejected by the EU Council (CRR, Art. 459).

What remains surprising from level playing field perspective is that the requirements to set institution-specific capital and systemic risk buffers are fully left to the member states (CRD IV, Arts 128-140) , as are the requirements to set macro-prudential buffers (CRR, Art. 458). In the EU context, such capacity should have been left to a central authority, such as EBA, or the ECB in the context of the Banking Union. It is only in exceptional circumstances that they need to be authorised by the EU Council.

The capital requirements for banks have thus increased importantly, which was one obvious lesson of the financial crisis: they should have been higher. This can already be noticed from the available data. Figure 6 shows a gradual increase in the Tier 1 ratios from 2008 onwards.

Figure 6. Evolution of Tier 1 capital ratios

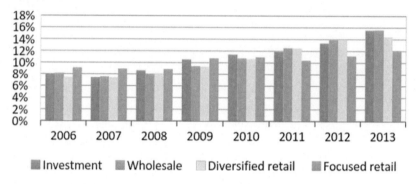

Note: The amounts expressed in the figure are median values of Tier 1 capital ratios, Tier 1 capital as percentage of risk-weighted assets.
Source: Ayadi & De Groen (2014).

All the binding capital ratios and buffers remain risk-weighted. A weakness thereby is that a preferential risk weight applies to some assets under the standardised ratings-based (SRB) approach. For example, the risk weight for government bonds is 0%, whereas reduced risk-weightings apply for mortgage debt depending on the level of collateral, and for loans to small and medium-sized enterprise (SME) the risk weights are multiplied by a factor 0.7619. The exposures to governments are further amplified due to an exemption from the large exposures limitation. Hence, CRD IV puts a €150-million, or 25% of own funds, cap on exposures to a single debtor. Government debt denominated in national currency, however, is excluded from the scope of these requirements. The largest euro area banks held at the end of 2013 government debt equivalent to about twice their own funds, of which almost 60% was debt from home-country governments (De Groen, 2015).

The banks can also choose to use the internal ratings-based (IRB) approach, an option used especially by the larger banks. This approach provides banks the possibility to use internal models to calibrate the probabilities of default and loss-given default, which form the foundation for the risk weights. The risk-weighted assets calibration is more costly under the IRB approach, i.e. in addition to the development and maintenance the internal models, additional reporting is required. These costs, however, are more than compensated by the reduction in capital charge-related costs. Banks need to require permission from the competent authority before they can use the IRB approach (CRR, Art. 143).

A major problem for supervisors is the erosion of risk-weighted assets under the internal ratings-based approach, and the differences applied by large banks in the risk weights for assets. For large banks, the EU average risk-weighting of assets is 33%, while in the US it is about 58%. This means that for these EU banks assets can be risk-weighted at one-third of the standard rule of 8% capital to total assets. A review by the Basel Committee found that internal risk weights for credit risk in the banking book vary significantly across banks, variations that are not necessarily supported by differences in underlying assets.

Capital ratios vary by as much as 1.5 to 2 percentage points in either direction around the 10% benchmark as a result of different practices (Basel Committee, 2013). The culprits of this situation are EU-based banks, accounting for over 40% of global bank assets, which can continue to be more or less 'compliant' with the Basel framework, while on average being highly leveraged. The average leverage ratio for large euro area banks was about 3.2%, or one percentage point below large US-based banks, even on a comparable IFRS basis (ECB, 2013, p. 39).

In addition, most EU-based banks that use the IRB approach, apply it to only part of their portfolio, invoking the 'permanent partial use', whereby they may request to follow rules of the standardised approach for certain exposures. Most notable are the zero risk-weighted government bond exposures (CRR, Arts 149-150). The EU regulation thus allows banks to 'cherry-pick' how they measure their risk: for sovereign exposure, banks can use the standardised approach, which assigns a risk of zero to all government bonds of euro area countries if they are denominated in euro (Gros, 2013). Another crucial exemption to the capital rules relates to bank insurance groups. The rules allow banks not to deduct from their common equity participations in insurance undertakings, under certain conditions (CRR, Art. 471).

Figure 7. Relationship between Z-score on distance to default and RWA

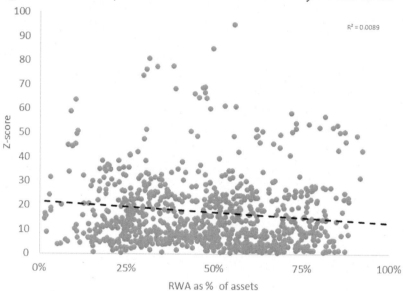

Notes: The axes have been cut at a Z-score of 1 to 100 and RWA to total assets to make it easier to visualise the large majority of the observations.

Source: Ayadi & De Groen (2014).

Notwithstanding the strengthening of the capital requirements, the calibration of the risk-weighted assets has not changed under CRD IV. Das & Sy (2012), for example, show that banks with lower average risk weights are not predicting well the market risk measures. Moreover, using the Z-score distance to default measure as an indicator for underlying risks reveals a misalignment with the risk-weighted assets. As shown in Figure 7 there seems to be no clear relation between the Z-score and the average risk-weighted assets. Using a multivariate regression finds that the relation is especially distorted for the banks that are more involved in financial markets activities and inter-bank activities (Ayadi et al., 2011 and 2014).

The only non-risk weighted ratio that is part of CRD IV is the leverage ratio, which is not binding for the time being. The CRR sets the way of calculating the ratio for reporting purposes, but does not make it obligatory, nor does it set a floor (CRR, Art. 429). This is left to an EBA report to be finalised by October 2016, which could be accompanied by a legislative proposal (CRR, Art. 450).

5.3 Liquidity

The rules on a minimum liquidity buffer to cope with (deposit) outflows are another important novelty of Basel III. Although banks are known for their maturity mismatch, prior legislation did not take into account the liquidity shortage that could trigger defaults. The new rules define liquid asset classes and set a minimum level. Under the former regime, no well-defined rules existed on liquidity, neither at global nor EU level. Under CRD I, it was left to the host country to set liquidity requirements, including for branches of other member states' banks, and was a matter of supervisory discretion.

The new rules on liquidity are contained in Art. 510 of the CRR, and were further detailed by an EBA Implementing Technical Standard (ITS). They require the holding of liquid to high-quality liquid assets (HQLA) to cover stressed conditions over a period of 30 days. The asset classes are subdivided in three categories: Level 1 (0% haircut): coins and bank notes, central bank reserves, 0% risk weighted (RW) debt securities issued or guaranteed by public entities, certain non-0% RW sovereign debt or central bank obligations issued in the country in which the liquidity risk is taken; Level 2A (15% haircut): 20% RW debt securities issued or guaranteed by sovereigns, central banks, PSEs, supranationals or MDBs, corporate debt securities rated at least AA and covered bonds not issued by the bank itself or any of its affiliates and rated AA minimum; Level 2B (25% to 50% haircut): certain residential mortgage-backed securities (RMBS) rated AA or higher, corporate debt securities rated A+ to BBB and unencumbered equities.

5.4 Reporting

The regulation also introduces reporting standards, which must reduce the information gap or so-called 'information asymmetry' between the bank and its supervisors. Financial reporting consists of the financial reporting for supervisory purposes known as FINREP, which is complemented by the reporting for capital requirements and own funds known as COREP. The reporting standards are designed by EBA under the various delegated acts, which have contributed to the harmonisation of definitions and methodologies. However, differences in accounting standards, as the basis for supervisory reporting, and in the enforcement of these standards persists. The majority of the directly supervised banks are reporting in IFRS, while some non-listed banks report in local and US GAAP, which can result in differences that make the data incomparable. The difference in the level of total assets under different accounting standards has, for instance, an impact on the leverage ratio as well as on the calibration of other micro- and macro-regulatory requirements. The accounting standards within the EU have converged in the past few years, at least for listed firms, while the talks between EU and US authorities to make IFRS and US GAAP compatible are stuck.

Besides reporting to the supervisor on the different regulatory capital and liquidity ratios, banks are also obliged to disclose additional information fields that seemingly have little to do with prudential affairs, e.g. tax and subsidy allocation as well as remuneration, to the public. The objective of the members of parliament who mainly pushed for the reporting on taxation and remuneration is to discipline the banks by granting the public the possibility to spot tax avoidance and excessive remuneration. The remuneration is further restricted by a cap on bank bonuses. The variable part of the remuneration is in principle limited at 100% of the fixed part. Only if shareholders agree can the ceiling be doubled to 200% (CRD IV, Art. 94). On the other hand, some member states have decided to apply more stringent requirements to the relative share of variable remuneration. For example, the Netherlands applies a cap of 20%.

5.5 Conclusions

The new EU bank capital framework substantially increases capital charges for banks, and above all for large banks. The paradigm has shifted: today, the larger the bank, the higher the level of capital. Formerly, this relationship was the reverse. Basel II was thus corrected for one of its important weaknesses, which had considerably contributed to the financial crisis. But two caveats remain: 1) the ratio is based upon a risk-weighting of assets, whereby under external models limited or no risk-weighting applies to important asset classes, and internal models are still allowed, although their robustness is questionable; 2) the capital buffers for large and systemically important banks are decided by the member states, who can still favour national champions. Hence much will depend on the consistent implementation to ensure the robustness of the new framework.

The new capital framework is furthermore composed of a host of measures, and also exemptions, which make the rules extremely complex to implement, raising the question of whether a simpler set of rules would have been preferable. The introduction of a leverage ratio by 2018 should allow for a simpler metric to judge banks' soundness. But a further streamlining of the rules, and a reduction of the exemptions, should be a priority in view of a more integrated banking market.

References

Ayadi, R., E. Arbak and W.P. De Groen (2011), "Business Models in European Banking: A pre-and post-crisis screening", Centre for European Policy Studies (CEPS), Brussels.

Ayadi, R. and W.P. De Groen (2014), *Banking Business Models Monitor 2014: Europe*, Paperback jointly published by Centre for European Policy Studies and International Observatory on Financial Service Cooperatives, Brussels and Montreal (www.ceps.be/book/banking-business-models-monitor-2014-europe).

Basel Committee (2013), "Analysis of risk-weighted assets for credit risk in the banking book", Regulatory Consistency Assessment Programme (RCAP), Bank for International Settlements, July.

Das, S. and A.N.R. Sy (2012), "How Risky Are Banks' Risk Weighted Assets? Evidence from the Financial Crisis", IMF Working Paper No. WP/12/36, International Monetary Fund, Washington, D.C.

De Groen, W.P. (2014), "Was the ECB's Comprehensive Assessment up to standard?", CEPS Policy Brief, CEPS, Brussels, March (www.ceps.eu/book/was-ecb%E2%80%99s-comprehensive-assessment-standard).

_____ (2015), "The ECB's QE: Time to break the doom loop between banks and their governments", CEPS Policy Brief, CEPS, Brussels, March (www.ceps.eu/book/ecb%E2%80%99s-qe-time-break-doom-loop-between-banks-and-their-governments).

De Nederlandsche Bank (DNB) (2013), CRD IV Academy.

European Central Bank (ECB) (2013), "Bank Structures Report", Frankfurt, November.

Gros, D. (2013), "Banking Union with a Sovereign Virus, The self-serving regulatory treatment of sovereign debt in the euro area", CEPS Policy Brief, CEPS, Brussels, March.

6. THE ECB AS BANK SUPERVISOR UNDER THE SINGLE SUPERVISORY MECHANISM*

Institutionally, the biggest change brought about by the financial and economic crisis was the decision to centralise banking supervision in the hands of the European Central Bank (ECB) . This seemed new in 2012, but the issue had actually been widely debated in the run-up to and during the first years of monetary union, as the possibility had already been foreseen in the Maastricht Treaty. The ECB, especially its Executive Board member Tommaso Padoa-Schioppa, had also pushed for it, but the EU finance ministers thought differently, until the decentralised structure of supervision in the EU proved untenable.[52]

Politically, the Single Supervisory Mechanism (SSM) was packaged under the Banking Union project, which was proposed in the Four Presidents Report, led by European Council President Van Rompuy (June 2012).[53] The two other Banking Union pillars are a resolution mechanism and a deposit insurance scheme that are discussed in the next chapter.

A banking union can be defined as a fully integrated bank regulatory and supervisory system within a federal structure. Supervision is denationalised, in that its form becomes exactly the same and is neutral with respect to the nationality of the bank. Banking unions exist today in other federations, such as in Canada, the US, Australia and even Germany and Switzerland. It is worth recalling that in these federations other elements of financial

---

* This chapter is a revised and updated version of Lannoo (2014).

[52] See e.g. the speech by Tommaso Padoa-Schioppa on EMU and banking supervision (Padoa-Schioppa, 1999) and the ECB paper (ECB, 2001).

[53] Van Rompuy et al. (2012).

supervision, such as the supervision of securities markets and insurance companies, or the taxation of firms and financial products, are not necessarily unified. Full federal supervision of banks does not mean that lower-level authorities no longer exercise competences, as is exemplified in the US.

In the EU model, a banking union, further to the Eurozone Council decision of June 2012, was formed on the basis of Art. 127(6) of the EU Treaty (TFEU). Hence, supervision moved to the ECB only for banks licensed in the eurozone, as that article is only applicable to those countries that are part of the EMU, not to the countries that have a derogation or a special status within the EU.

Art. 127.6 (TFEU) reads:

> The Council, acting by means of regulations in accordance with a special legislative procedure, may unanimously, and after consulting the European Parliament and the European Central Bank, confer specific tasks upon the European Central Bank concerning policies relating to the prudential supervision of credit institutions and other financial institutions with the exception of insurance undertakings.

This language is repeated in Art. 25 of the European System of Central Banks (ESCB) Statute.

The Regulation implementing the SSM was adopted in October 2013 and formed the basis for the ECB to start as banking supervisor in November 2014. This chapter discusses the key aspects of the SSM: its composition and operational structure, the supervisory reporting and division of labour between the ECB and national authorities, the European Banking Authority (EBA) and the European Systemic Risk Board (ESRB).

6.1   The basis: The SSM Regulation

The SSM Regulation is a relatively straightforward piece of EU legislation implementing Art. 127(6) of the EU Treaty. It supersedes the home/host-country distinction and entrusts to the ECB authorisation and supervision of the systemic and largest credit institutions of each of the eurozone countries and of the countries that choose to opt in to the SSM. It defines supervision, mandates cooperation between the ECB and the national competent authorities (NCAs), the other European Supervisory Authorities (ESAs) and the ESRB. It allows the ECB to enact regulations and guidelines to carry out the tasks set out in the SSM Regulation. For those credit institutions in the eurozone where the ECB is not in charge of direct supervision, the regulation maintains the home/host-country system (Art. 17) but mandates close cooperation with and reporting to the ECB. It also allows the ECB to take over supervision of those institutions at any time (Art. 6.5b).

The SSM only covers prudential supervision. The regulation states clearly that those "supervisory tasks not conferred on the ECB should remain with the national authorities" (Recital 28). Nor are accounting standards harmonised by the Regulation (Recital 19). In addition, capital buffers and macro-prudential measures remain the primary responsibility of the member states, as further to the capital requirements Directive (CRD IV), implementing Basel III, although the ECB is allowed to apply higher buffers (Art. 5.1-2).

Soon after publication of the SSM Regulation, the ECB published a list of the 130 institutions falling under its direct supervision, and announced a comprehensive assessment of these institutions, as foreseen in Art. 33.4, "prior to assuming its new supervisory tasks in November 2014" (see Figure 18). This list included all banks that the ECB believed could be regarded as significant at that time, when the methodology to determine significance had not been finalised. This comprised an asset quality review (AQR) and a stress test. The intention of the exercise was to increase transparency, build confidence and repair the banking system where necessary, requiring corrective measures from the banks. The Common Equity Tier 1 (CET1) capital was used as a benchmark, with a threshold level of 8% for the AQR and baseline scenario of the stress test, and 5.5% for the adverse scenario. In total, 25 banks failed at least one part of the test, in total falling €24.6 billion short (see ECB, 2014e). Due to capital measures taken earlier in 2014 and restructuring arrangements agreed with the European Commission, only eight of the banks still had to raise in total €6 billion in the period up to July 2015.

The list was later narrowed down to 120 banking groups, the 'significant' banks, accounting for almost 85% of total banking assets in the euro area, and published jointly with the list of 'less significant' banks on 4 September 2014. The list illustrates the huge diversity of banking models and structures in Europe, with France having four large banks with assets in excess of €1 trillion, compared to only one in Germany (see Figure 8). But the latter country has a long list of less significant banks.

Figure 8. Distribution of assets of the 10 largest banks supervised by the ECB in five countries, 2013

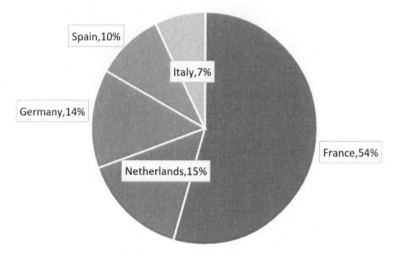

Source: CEPS.

The diversity is also clear from a distinction on the basis of ownership (see Figure 9). The single largest group are public limited or commercial banks (SHV). This group accounts for about two-fifths of the banks supervised by the ECB, including subsidiaries of both EEA non-SSM and non-EEA banks. Cooperative and savings banks each represent almost one-fifth of the banks supervised by the ECB. The third group, accounting for the remaining fifth, are public banks and banks nationalised during the crisis. This diversity highlights what a challenge the ECB has in putting in place an "independent, intrusive and forward-looking supervision", in the words of Danièle Nouy, Chair of the Supervisory Board of the Single Supervisory Mechanism, writing in the SSM's first Annual Report (ECB, 2015).

Figure 9. Banks supervised by the ECB by type of ownership

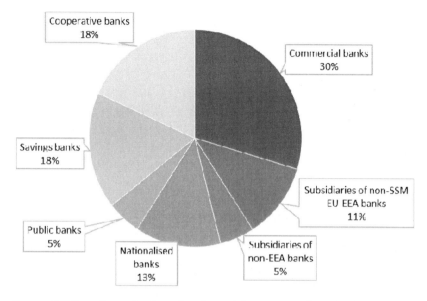

Source: CEPS configuration based on financial statements from banks under the SSM.

6.2 The SSM operational structure

Merging 18 different supervisory authorities into one operational structure is a monumental task. Not only does it pose pure operational challenges, but also political and cultural ones. It is not unprecedented in the history of European integration – the start of monetary union in 1994 with the European Monetary Institute was a comparable effort – but the lead time was much longer, in the context of a smaller EU and EMU. The SSM's first Annual Report gives a good overview of the operational challenges (ECB, 2015).

The central elements of the SSM operational structure are the Supervisory Board and the Joint Supervisory Teams. The Supervisory Board is composed of a chair, a vice-chair, four ECB representatives, the representatives of all of the NCAs and the eventual opt-ins, which have equal voting rights. The Supervisory Board, however, is subordinate to the ECB's Governing Council, which has ultimate decision-making power, and in which the opt-ins are not represented. The concerns of the opt-ins may thus not be sufficiently taken into account. An appeals process is foreseen in a decision by the ECB's Governing Council for opt-ins, but they do not have a full say.

Opt-ins have an additional disadvantage, i.e. they cannot take part in the liquidity-providing operations of the ECB, unless they have substantial operations and collateral in the eurozone. Moreover, as long as the opt-ins are not part of the euro area, the risk that they may opt out again will hinder their financial institutions. Hence, even if the facility of opting in to the SSM is a good way to bridge the gap between the ins and the outs, the playing field remains uneven.

The Supervisory Board is assisted by a Steering Committee, which is responsible for preparing its meetings. The Supervisory Board has a more limited composition and follows a rotational system, to ensure a balanced composition of NCAs. But it has no formal decision-making capacity.

The Joint Supervisory Teams (JSTs) should be the big game changer of the SSM. These teams are in charge of the day-to-day supervision of those banks that are the responsibility of the ECB. They are composed of ECB and NCA representatives. They replace, at least for the SSM, the function of the Colleges of Supervisors of banks active exclusively in SSM countries, and should ensure a more balanced, more efficient and less biased supervision of cross-border banks. Their size and composition varies depending upon the supervised institutions.

The chair as well as the core team (except sub-coordinators) are part of the ECB staff, and the full team are a combination of local and international staff from the ECB and NCAs. The chair cannot come from the same country as the home country of the bank. He/she can delegate specific tasks and liaise with sub-coordinators of the NCAs. The SSM Regulation states that the "exchange and secondment of staff should establish a common supervisory culture", on which the ECB should report on a regular basis (Recital 79). Danièle Nouy, Chair of the ECB Supervisory Board, announced further details of the JSTs on 30 September 2014: "We will be a truly pan-European supervisor operating without national bias or prejudice." For example, she indicated that Crédit Agricole's chief supervisor will be a German national, Unicredit's French and ABN AMRO's Spanish.

The composition of the JSTs was further detailed in the April 2014 ECB Regulation and in the September 2014 Banking Supervision Guide (see Figure 10). These documents state that the ECB is in charge of the establishment and the composition of JSTs, and that it can modify the appointments made by NCAs (Art. 4, ECB Regulation). JSTs are appointed for a period of three to five years, depending on the risk profile and complexity of the institution. JST coordinators and members are expected to rotate on a regular basis. The challenge is to acquire the necessary expertise about the 120 banks in the ECB, compose balanced and competent teams, make the JSTs work effectively together, and avoid duplication of effort between the NCAs. The human resource management skills of the ECB are thus be crucial.

Figure 10. Organisational pyramid of the Joint Supervisory Teams

- Established for every banking group, comprising staff from ECB and NCA
- Responsible for day-to-day supervision of individual significant institutions and for implementing the annual supervisory programme
- Responsible for implementing decisions of Supervisory Board/Governing Council
- Size and composition of JSTs vary between institutions

Source: ECB (2014c), "Guide to Banking Supervision", p. 16.

Whereas supervisory colleges were already multinational, the big change for the SSM is the single centre, the ECB. Previously, the home country was in charge of final supervision, with reporting lines from host-country authorities that EU-wide resembled a spaghetti. Under the new model, the ECB appoints the members of the Supervisory College and serves as chair for the banks for which it acts as consolidating supervisor. The members from NCAs within the SSM can participate as observers. For significant banks from outside the SSM, the ECB participates in the College as member, and the NCAs as observers (Art. 10, ECB Regulation). The challenge is to make the transition to the new structure as fluid as possible, avoiding abrupt changes and the imposition of too many new requirements on banks, in order to achieve the ultimate goal: adequate supervision.

A key element for the JSTs and the SSM is the language regime. As a general rule, the supervised entities may address the ECB in any one of the official languages of the EU. Decisions addressed to supervised entities are adopted in English and the official language of the home member state. The ECB nevertheless allows banks to use only one official EU language in their written communications, including with regard to ECB supervisory decisions (Art. 24, ECB Regulation). For communications between the ECB and the NCAs, English is used as a rule, although it is not the standard for most NCAs and supervisors in the member states, and presents a big challenge for the functioning of the JST, as an enormous amount of relevant information on the supervised entities is available only in the national language.

With a view to ensuring a fluid transition, the ECB will need to be pragmatic, with core documents in English, and supporting documents in the home-country language of the bank. This means that most banks in the SSM, of which only two countries use English as the official language (Ireland and Malta), need to move to dual-language documentation, which is a huge challenge. But once the system becomes truly functional, it will be a big step forward towards a common supervisory culture and equally for a common understanding of reporting and data.

The costs incurred by the ECB for the SSM and its supervisory activities are paid for by contributions from all the SSM banks, following the SSM Regulation (Art. 30). The ECB estimated that this amounts to about €260 million for 2015. A draft paper was circulated, setting out the methodology for calculating the contributions. This does not impact the respective national systems, where the cost of supervision is accounted for in different ways. Many banks thus end up paying over and above the national contributions.

6.3 Common definitions for supervisory reporting and data processing

A prerequisite for an SSM and the JSTs are common definitions for supervisory reporting and an integrated IT infrastructure. Here, the ECB can build on the work undertaken jointly with the EBA in recent years. But unravelling and assessing the progress achieved in this domain is not a trivial task and challenges remain. In addition, as supervisory reporting is related to financial reporting and to the IT framework used, allegiance to this framework must be maintained to avoid duplication and confusion.

Harmonised reporting requirements are required by CRD IV, but work on the subject started well before, with the financial reporting (FINREP) and common reporting (COREP) work of the EBA and its predecessor CEBS in 2006. FINREP introduces standardised data formats and definitions for financial reporting for prudential purposes, which use International Financial Reporting Standards (IFRS) templates. This is complemented by COREP for reporting of the capital adequacy and own funds ratios, as set forward in CRD IV. The aim is to provide supervisors with all relevant information on the financial institutions' risk exposure, as well as their capital and liquidity positions. COREP and FINREP use Extended Business Reporting Language (XBRL) that sets a common taxonomy for financial reporting, compatible with IFRS.

Initially, the supervisory reporting framework gave too much flexibility to national supervisors, as it was too accommodating to the different national reporting formats, which was clear from the huge number of cells through which banks could report core (1,277 cells) and detailed (21,606 cells) prudential information. The maximum number of cells that banks could be asked to use was about 18,000, as not all information was applicable to all banks at the same time (CEBS, 2006). On top of that, COREP and FINREP were implemented to varying degrees across member states (see ECB, 2010, p. 62).

The financial crisis, CRD IV and the advent of the SSM galvanised an in-depth review of COREP and FINREP, which led to the Commission Implementing Regulation No. 680/2014 on supervisory reporting. But it also contained an extension towards large exposures, leverage, liquidity, stable funding, asset encumbrance, forbearance and non-performing exposures. The Regulation uses a Data Point Model to reconcile different reporting frameworks with their respective IT solutions, with a view towards avoiding unjustified implementation and operating costs, so as to ensure that the different IT solutions in place produce harmonised data as well as reliable data quality. The 2014 Supervisory Reporting Regulation follows maximum harmonisation, and has not reduced the number of reporting cells, but made the data formats identical across member states.

But much of this remains work in progress. Amendments were proposed in July 2014 to the 2014 Supervisory Reporting Regulation covering non-performing exposures (NPE) and forbearance. A non-performing exposure is defined as every material exposure that is 90 days past due even if it is not recognised as in default or impaired. But this does not impact the payment cycles in EU member states, which vary widely (from one to four months). In August 2014, the EBA also published a new XBRL taxonomy to be used by competent authorities for remittance of data under the EBA Implementing Technical Standards (ITS) on supervisory reporting. It replaces the existing one that was released in September 2013.

The ECB's October 2014 Asset Quality Review used the latest definitions on NPE of the EBA, resulting in a much higher level of NPE provisions than before. Overall, 28% of the banks used an NPE definition that was less conservative than the AQR, compared to 15% that used a more conservative definition, leading to an increase of €55 billion on the NPE book. This added up to €81 billion as a consequence of the credit file review in the context of the AQR, resulting in an additional €136 billion in provisions. The overall increases among SSM debtor countries ranged from 7% to 116%, with the largest percentage increases for shipping finance, but in terms of volume, the most was for large SMEs and corporate finance, followed by real estate (ECB, 2014e, p. 67).

The relationship with IFRS forms an additional difficulty that was clearly brought to the fore by the financial crisis (see Nouy, 2014). The IFRS relies heavily on fair-value accounting, but this only provides useful information for certain liquid financial assets and liabilities. For various other items on a bank's balance sheet, there is no market information. For these items, the use of fair value reduces both the verifiability and comparability of the results. Second, accounting standards allow for a delayed recognition of credit losses on loans and debt instruments or 'impairment charges', as they require observable indicators that signal a default of the counterparty. Third, there was no accounting rule for off-balance sheet exposures, such as for Special Purpose Entities (SPEs). At the request of the G-20, the International Accounting Standards Board has already come up with improved rules on fair-value recognition and additional disclosure towards SPEs, and is working on a model for more timely recognition of credit losses. But a downside is the continued divergence between the EU and the US on global accounting rules.

More will have to be done to maintain the link between IFRS and supervisory reporting. In a speech on accounting and financial reporting for central banks, Danielle Nouy asked standard setters to consider the financial stability implications of any revisions to existing accounting rules or when developing new ones and to identify, analyse and – where feasible – mitigate the potential pro-cyclical effects of financial reporting. But, more important, she insisted that the ECB wanted to continue to use financial reporting standards as a basis for supervisory reporting (see Nouy, 2014). This has two important implications: i) internationally, progress must be achieved towards a single accounting standard, while improving the quality of the standards, and ii) within Europe, the use of IFRS must be broadened, which is not required for non-listed corporations, including many of the 120 banks the ECB supervises.

The ECB therefore launched a consultation in October 2014 to extend the uniform supervisory financial reporting requirement (FINREP, based upon IFRS) to a significant number of supervised groups applying national generally accepted accounting principles (GAAP), taking proportionality into account. In the AQR, the ECB already made valuation adjustments for €4.6 billion to the banks supervised by the ECB as a result of the fair-value exposures review (ECB, 2014e, p. 93). This implies that the ECB *de facto* already started to apply one standard, even if the SSM Regulation explicitly states that accounting standards do not fall within its reach (Recital 19).

6.4   Supervisory tasks of the ECB and NCAs

The split between the ECB and NCAs is twofold: the ECB supervises the significant institutions of the participating states of the SSM, and only in the prudential field. Supervision of the other institutions and the other tasks are left to the NCAs. Or to express the arrangement differently, the original EU form of supervision continues to apply where the ECB is not the supervisor, with the ordinary division of competences between home- and host-country supervisors. But some important exceptions to the ECB's competences are set in CRD IV and the capital requirements Regulation (CRR), and in the draft 'Barnier' proposals on the structure of banks. The ECB can mandate NCAs to cooperate closely with the ECB and override their decisions in its fields of competence, but evidence will need to indicate how this will function. This may even be more difficult towards the non-eurozone countries that opt-in to the SSM (see Table 6 for an overview of the relevant prudential supervisors for credit institutions and branches).

The division of labour for 'passporting' between the ECB and the NCAs is a more complex process than indicated above, and was detailed in the ECB's SSM Framework Regulation (April 2014) and the Guide to Banking Supervision (September 2014). The passporting procedure continues even for the significant banks to follow EU law, i.e. a bank wishing to provide services or to set up a branch in another SSM or non-SSM state needs to inform its NCA, who then informs the ECB (Arts 11-12, SSM Framework Regulation). For banks from non-participating states, the same applies. The ECB thus exercises the powers of the home- and host-member state. One may wonder whether it still makes sense to maintain the detour of the notification to NCAs for significant banks within the eurozone.

Table 6. Relevant prudential supervisors for credit institutions/branches in the EEA

Type of bank	Area in which credit institution/branch is located				
	Euro area (SSM)	Other EU		Other EEA (Non-SSM)	Third (Non-SSM)
		SSM	Non-SSM		
Parent credit institution domiciled in SSM area					
Significant (Group)	ECB	ECB	..	..	..
- *Subsidiary*	ECB	ECB	NCA	NCA	NCA
- *Branch*	ECB	ECB	ECB	ECB	NCA
Less significant (Group)	NCA/ECB	NCA/ECB	..	..	..
- *Subsidiary*	NCA/ECB	NCA/ECB	NCA	NCA	NCA
- *Branch*	(F)NCA/ECB	(F)NCA/ECB	FNCA/ECB	FNCA/ECB	NCA
Parent credit institution domiciled in non-SSM EEA area					
Signif. & less-signif. (Group)	..	..	NCA	NCA	..
- *Subsidiary (Signif.)*	ECB	ECB	NCA	NCA	NCA
- *Subsidiary (Less-signif.)*	NCA/ECB	NCA/ECB	NCA	NCA	NCA
- *Branch*	FNCA	FNCA	(F)NCA	(F)NCA	FNCA
Parent credit institution domiciled in non-EEA area					
Signif. & less-signif. (Group)	..	..	..	..	NCA
- *Subsidiary (Signif.)*	ECB	ECB	NCA	NCA	NCA
- *Subsidiary (Less-signif.)*	NCA/ECB	NCA/ECB	NCA	NCA	NCA
- *Branch*	..	..	..	..	NCA

Notes: Significant institutions are credit institutions that have more than €30 billion in assets; represent more than 20% of GDP and at least €5 billion in assets; are among the three largest credit institutions in the member state; or have more than significant cross-border assets. The grey highlights the areas in which the SSM contributed to a change in supervision. NCA = national competent authority; FNCA = foreign national competent authority.

Source: Author's own compilation.

Although CRD IV was negotiated at the same time that the SSM initiative was launched, it leaves important prudential supervisory tasks explicitly to NCAs. CRD IV and the CRR make explicit reference to "Member States", as compared to "competent authorities", regarding the determination of capital buffers, macro-prudential buffers or the reduced weightings for mortgage debt. The requirements for setting institution-specific capital and systemic risk buffers are fully left to the member states (CRD IV, Arts 128-140), as are the requirements for setting macro-prudential buffers (CRR, Art. 458). But the freedom left to member states is clearly defined, and the Council has the power to reject the proposed national macro-prudential measures in accordance with Article 291 TFEU (Implementing Acts), acting on a proposal by the Commission.

Reduced risk-weightings for mortgage debt apply under the external ratings-based or standardised approach of Basel II (CRD IV, Art. 124). The general rule is a 35% risk-weighting for loans secured by residential property and 50% for commercial property, but "member states" can ask for more rigorous criteria for the assessment of the mortgage lending value in statutory or regulatory provisions. In this case, however, the attribution of these competences is not so clear in the article as it is for the capital buffers, as it refers mostly to "competent authorities". A higher risk weight will be set based on loss experience and taking into account forward-looking markets developments and financial stability considerations, and be based on EBA standards. Host-country rules apply in case of cross-border activity.

The SSM Regulation allows the ECB to set higher requirements for capital buffers and macro-prudential risks than those laid down in the CRD IV, and "any national competent authority" can ask the ECB to act in this sense (Art. 5 (2)(3)). The ECB, when doing so, shall cooperate closely with the NCAs. It needs to notify the member state in question and state the reasons. In doing so, the ECB needs to take the specific situation of the member state into account.

Other elements of the CRD IV fall in a grey zone between the ECB and the NCAs, such as for example the leverage and liquidity coverage ratio (LCR), until they will be fully implemented in 2018. In the meantime, member states may impose national requirements or require a faster transition. In the Netherlands, for example, a 4% leverage ratio by 2018 was imposed as a 'Pillar II' issue, which falls under the discretion of the supervisor. The LCR will fully apply from 2018 onwards, but its application to branches is a host-country competence; hence, the NCAs will regulate, meaning again that no single rule exists. Overall, the ECB indicated, in response to a question from a member of the European Parliament, there are some 150 legal provisions where flexibility is expressly granted either to the competent authorities (that is, the supervisory authority) or to the national government for the application of prudential requirements to European Union banks.[54]

Under the Barnier (or Liikanen) proposal on the structure of banking (European Commission, 2014c), the ECB may have an additional but delicate supervisory task, if adopted, which is to require large banks to separate their trading activities from their ordinary deposit-taking and lending business. The draft prohibits proprietary trading, but allows trading for market making, hedging and underwriting purposes. The draft leaves this task with the "competent authorities", but will this be the ECB under the SSM?

This could apply for Global SIFIs, and for banks having trading activities above a certain threshold. The ECB, or the NCAs outside the SSM, would have to review the permissible trading activities of such banks, and if they find that some pose a threat to financial stability, they could require the institution to separate its entities into a banking group. But derogation from this requirement could be requested by the member states for national legislation adopted before January 2014, to be approved by the European Commission (Art. 21). Hence these member states would need to lobby the Commission for their legislation on banking structures to be accepted before the ECB imposes separation. The French, German and British legislation on the subject, all adopted before the Commission proposal, do not go as far as Europe has gone, or call for a different form of separation.

---

[54] Letter from Danièle Nouy, Chair of the Supervisory Board, to several Members of the European Parliament, on options and national discretions, 26 May 2015.

6.5 Division of labour between the ECB and the EBA

The division of labour, at least within the SSM, seems to be clear-cut: the ECB is in charge of prudential supervision, and the EBA is the standard setter. However, the split is not so precise. The EBA also has supervisory tasks, such as data collection, stress tests and participation in supervisory colleges, whereas the ECB can adopt its own rules. Moreover, the ECB is not formally represented on the EBA board; this remains exclusively the role of the member states. These issues are also relevant for the other ESAs, and the entire European System of Financial Supervisors (ESFS), and in particular for the ESRB, although the latter's secretariat is based within the ECB.

The Regulation governing the EBA was modified at the same time that the SSM was adopted. It basically changes the voting procedures in the Board of Supervisors to allow for a positive co-existence between the SSM members and non-members, requiring qualified majorities in both groups for measures adopted by the EBA. The Regulation also allows a representative of the ECB's Supervisory Board to participate in the EBA Board of Supervisors, without a right to vote, and to attend discussions within the Board of Supervisors relating to individual financial institutions (Art. 44.4). The ECB is thus not formally represented as a supervisor within the EBA.

Confusion may emerge in markets concerning who is in charge, and duplication in reporting by banks can be an issue. The EBA conducted its 2014 stress tests on 123 banks, which were not an entirely comparable sample of banks and using different configurations of banking groups from the 130 banks on which the ECB was applying its comprehensive assessment. The end result was well-coordinated, using the same methodology and the same data formats, and was welcomed by the markets, but duplication may have occurred in reporting, at least for the banks supervised by the ECB, and some resistance could emerge, also towards future stress tests. Hence extensive coordination between both organisations should continue to be a priority.

Other supervisory tasks of EBA include the participation in supervisory colleges, conducting peer reviews of supervisors, mediating between supervisors and resolution authorities and delegating responsibilities. As regards the colleges, the EBA stresses that it will continue to play an important role in colleges where the consolidating supervisor is outside the SSM. Some 105 colleges were identified by the EBA during the course of 2013, of which 43 are being closely monitored. Some 73% of these are headquartered inside the SSM, and the remainder outside the SSM (19%) or in third countries (7%). The EBA says that "the number of colleges will be only slightly affected by the introduction of SSM" and "that only five banking groups will have presence only inside SSM countries". Hence "cross-border aspects in supervisory cooperation will remain significant also after SSM is in place" (EBA, 2014). In our view, the start of the SSM should allow for a significant decline in the number of statutory supervisors present in a college, and make supervision more consistent. On peer reviews, the question arises whether this also applies within the SSM, and to the ECB.

In its report on the ESAs, the European Commission did not address these or other sensitive matters. On the contrary, it recommended that "the focus on supervisory convergence could be increased", but without mentioning the role of the ECB under the SSM (European Commission, 2014a). It calls for swifter decision-making within the EBA, but without raising the issues of representation and the non-voting right of the ECB in the EBA and of the chair and managing directors of the EBA. On the budget, the Commission suggested revisiting the current financing arrangements of EBA, which is based on a 40% contribution of the EU budget and 60% from the member states, without recommending a specific change. In the Staff Working Document, however, it raises the possibility of contributions from the supervised institutions.

The European Parliament, in its report on the European System of Financial Supervisors (ESFS) , went much further, and called for a full review of respective regulations, covering as well the governance and the role of the chair, the powers of and the rule-making by the ESAs and the European Commission and the role of the ESRB within the ECB. As regards the EBA, it asked for a thorough assessment of its tasks and mandate in view of the start of the SSM (European Parliament, 2014). The Commission has thus chosen to duck the debate.

Confronted with a possible duplication of rule-making owing to the start of the SSM, the EBA and the European Commission, as the endorser of secondary legislation, should be extremely vigilant in monitoring and controlling the regulatory output. The establishment of the Single Rulebook is a noteworthy objective, but it could lead to an almost unstoppable process. In 2013-15, with the implementation of CRD IV/CRR, the EBA issued or is in the process of issuing 49 regulatory technical standards (RTSs) and 26 implementing technical standards (ITS). In a report for the European Parliament, experts called for a 'Structured Single Rulebook'. ESAs should apply a 'think-small principle' when developing new implementing measures and apply proportioned rules to small and medium-sized businesses. ESAs should also measure the impact of their proposals on other regulated entities and assess any unintended consequences on the EU economy (Demarigny et al., 2013). Others have called for more consistency across RTSs and ITSs, or to group them according to themes.

The problem is that the secondary legislative process is almost entirely under the control of the European Commission. The European Parliament and the Council have up to six months to react to an RTS, but they can only reject it if they do not agree with its implementation (Art. 13 EBA Regulation). On ITSs, there is no direct control by European Parliament and the Council. The huge volume of rule-making activity also raises the question of consistent implementation and application across the EU. Some level 2 acts are regulations, and thus directly applicable, whereas others are directives. The EBA and the European Commission have a Q&A for interpretation of level 2 legislation, which almost has the force of law, but this is not an ideal situation. Now that post-crisis rule-making is (almost) over, it is time to reconsider the effectiveness and appropriateness of the Single Rulebook objective. Inspiration could be drawn from the Regulatory Fitness and Performance (REFIT) exercise that is being applied in other areas of EU rule-making.

6.6 Division of labour between the ECB and ESRB

The possible duplication of tasks applies as well to the ESRB, but in this case, for an organisation based within the ECB. Everything depends on the effective cooperation established between the Supervisory Board of the SSM, which also has macro-prudential tasks, and the ESRB, which is not supposed to look at individual institutions in the member states. Here again, the Commission report on the functioning of the ESRB was silent on the division of competences with the SSM and the possible replication of tasks (European Commission, 2014b).

The broader questions are: What should macro-prudential regulation do, and should it be a task of the central bank? On the first question, a consensus exists that it should tackle systemic risk, smooth the financial cycle and limit contagion, but how and to what extent remain to be seen. Tackling certain indicators may not be sufficient, or may lead to strong reactions from certain interest groups. Hence the results will always be sub-optimal. Locating the function in a central bank raises the additional problem of whether macro-prudential considerations should be part of the monetary policy stance. Macro-prudential tasks could divert attention from the inflation target, create conflicts of interest or politicise the central bank. The Fed, as well as the ECB, have indicated that financial stability is the task of macro-prudential policy bodies, whereas interest-rate policy pursues macro-economic targets (Portes, 2014). The danger posed by deflation to financial stability, however, highlights that it is difficult to maintain a clear separation between both policies and makes it imperative that the central bank takes action, which is the view of the Bank for International Settlements (BIS). Or expressed the other way around, a deflationary environment will require even more action on the macro-prudential side. Hence the policies are complementary.

Locating the macro-prudential function within the ECB has fostered the necessary cooperation, which should also facilitate global coordination. Even under the SSM, member states and national designated authorities retain important competences, such as for financial stability and macro-prudential buffers (see e.g. CRR Art. 458) for banks, subject to coordination with EU bodies to avoid negative spillover effects. The ESRB highlights that implementing these macro-prudential instruments needs to be part of a strategy, and that they need to be coordinated. But the problem is that the ESRB, unlike, for example, the British Financial Policy Committee, can only issue recommendations on the subject. In 2011, the ESRB issued a recommendation to the national authorities to assign, in their national legislation, a single national macro-prudential body in charge of financial stability with a clear mandate, statute, means and structures to monitor and mitigate macro-prudential risks.

In the 2013 Annual Report, published in July 2014, the ESRB noted that there have been substantial delays in implementing this provision (ESRB, 2014, p. 56), and that the operationalisation of macro-prudential policy across the EU is in progress (ESRB, 2014, p. 49). One problem is that the tasks have been assigned to different authorities in the EU, mostly the central banks, but also the FSA and a separate committee (Schoenmaker, 2014). In addition, the ESRB complained that the data received from national authorities leave much to be desired. The problem with this situation is that the SSM, or the micro-prudential arm of the ECB, may take over the macro-prudential function, as it has clear powers to oversee and, if necessary, override NCAs, but only within the SSM.

Hence the future role of the ESRB within the ECB is unclear in the context of the SSM. On the one hand, it is a useful network to further the discussion on the policy framework for tackling macro-prudential risks within the EU as a whole, although other fora exist for this as well. On the other hand, the SSM also has macro-prudential competences, but only for the eurozone and opt-ins. The SSM side will have much more accurate and harmonised data, and more capacity to act. Of course, as with all micro-supervisors, the crucial question is whether it will see the bigger picture.

6.7 Conclusion

The ECB will have to maintain its credibility as a central bank, set a high standard as supervisor, and demonstrate that both tasks can be combined under one roof. The advantage of the combination is that the ECB will be much better informed than in the past about the state of the European financial system. The disadvantage is that it may blur its tasks, which may undermine the effectiveness of both policies. This could be aggravated by the complexity of the structure under which it has to work.

The basis for the SSM, as well as the operational structure, will need to be reviewed regularly. The legal base currently limits the ECB's tasks to prudential supervision of banks. However, the need may arise to expand these to insurance companies, or to capital market activities, which will evidently require an EU Treaty change.

At the same time, the suitability of the combination of monetary policy and supervisory functions under the same roof will have to be assessed continually.

References

CEBS (2006), "Framework for Common Reporting of the New Solvency Ratio", Committee of European Banking Supervisors, 13 January.

Constancio, V. (2014), "Banking Union: Meaning and implications for the future of banking", Paper prepared for Banking Union Conference organised by the Master in Banking and Financial Regulation, Navarra University, Madrid, 24 April.

De Groen, W.P. (2014), "Was the ECB's Comprehensive Assessment up to standard?", CEPS Policy Brief, Centre for European Policy Studies, Brussels (www.ceps.eu/node/9795).

De Groen, W.P. and K. Lannoo (2014), "The ECB AQR and the EBA Stress Test: What will the numbers tell?", CEPS Commentary, Centre for European Policy Studies, Brussels (www.ceps.eu/book/ecb-aqr-and-eba-stress-test-what-will-numbers-tell).

de Larosière, Jacques (2009), "Report of the High-Level Group on Financial Supervision in the EU", 25 February, Brussels.

Demarigny, F. et al. (2013), "Review of the New European System of Financial Supervision (ESFS)", Part 1, Document requested by the European Parliament's Committee on Economic and Monetary Affairs, October.

Dullien, S. (2014), "How to complete Europe's Banking Union", ECFR Policy Brief, European Council on Foreign Relations, London.

EBA and ECB (2014), "MFI Balance Sheet and Interest Rate Statistics, Securities Holdings Statistics and Implementing Technical Standards on Supervisory Reporting", April.

ECB (2001), "The role of central banks in prudential supervision", Note, 22, European Central Bank, Frankfurt, March.

_____ (2010), "MFI balance sheet and interest rate statistics and CEBS' guidelines on FINREP and COREP", Bridging Reporting Requirements Methodological Manual, European Central Bank, Frankfurt, February.

_____ (2013a), "Note: Comprehensive Assessment", European Central Bank, Frankfurt, October.

_____ (2014a), "Note on the Comprehensive Assessment", European Central Bank, Frankfurt, July.

_____ (2014b), Regulation of the European Central Bank of 16 April 2014 establishing the framework for cooperation within the Single Supervisory Mechanism between the European Central Bank and national competent authorities and with national designated authorities (SSM Framework Regulation), European Central Bank, Frankfurt.

_____ (2104c), "Guide to Banking Supervision", European Central Bank, Frankfurt, September.

_____ (2014d), "Financial Integration Report", European Central Bank, Frankfurt, April.

_____ (2014e), "Aggregate Report on the Comprehensive Assessment", European Central Bank, Frankfurt, October.

_____ (2015), "Annual Report on Supervisory Activities", European Central Bank, Frankfurt, March.

European Commission (2014a), Report from the Commission to the European Parliament and the Council on the operation of the European Supervisory Authorities (ESAs) and the European System of Financial Supervision (ESFS), August.

_____ (2014b), Report from the Commission to the European Parliament and the Council on the mission and organisation of the European Systemic Risk Board (ESRB).

_____ (2014c), Proposal for a Regulation of the European Parliament and of the Council on structural measures improving the resilience of EU credit institutions, January.

_____ (2014d), Commission Implementing Regulation (EU) No 680/2014 of 16 April 2014 laying down implementing technical standards with regard to supervisory reporting of institutions according to Regulation (EU) No 575/2013 of the European Parliament and of the Council.

European Parliament (2014), Report with recommendations to the Commission on the European System of Financial Supervision (ESFS) Review, February.

European Parliament and Council (2013), Regulation (EU) No 1022/2013 of the European Parliament and of the Council of 22 October 2013 amending Regulation (EU) No 1093/2010 establishing a European Supervisory Authority (European Banking Authority) as regards the conferral of specific tasks on the European Central Bank pursuant to Council Regulation (EU), No 1024/2013.

ESRB (2014a), 2013 Annual Report.

_____ (2014b), "Is Europe Overbanked?", Reports of the Advisory Scientific Committee, European Systemic Risk Board, June.

Gandrup, C. and M. Hallerberg (2014), "Supervisory Transparency in the European Banking Union", Bruegel Policy Contribution, Bruegel, Brussels.

Gros, D., C. Alcidi and A. Giovannini (2014), "Targeted longer-term refinancing operations (TLTROs): Will they revitalise credit in the euro area?", Report for the European Parliament's Committee on Economic and Monetary Affairs, Brussels, September.

Lannoo, K. (2014), *ECB Banking Supervision and Beyond*, CEPS Task Force Report, CEPS, Brussels.

Nouy, D. (2014), "Regulatory and financial reporting essential for effective banking supervision and financial stability", Speech at the fourth ECB Conference on Accounting, Financial Reporting and Corporate Governance for Central Banks, 3 July.

Padoa-Schioppa, T. (1999), "EMU and Banking Supervision", Speech at the London School of Economics, Financial Markets Group, London, 24 February.

Pagano, M. and G. Pica (2012), "Finance and employment", *Economic Policy*, 27(69): 5-55.

Portes, R. (2014), "Macro-Prudential Regulation in the SSM", Task Force Presentation at CEPS, mimeo, 4 July.

Schoenmaker, D., D. Gros, M. Pagano and S. Langfield (2014), "Allocating macro-prudential powers", Report of the Advisory Scientific Committee for the ESRB.

Valiante, D. (2014), "Framing banking union in a common currency area: Some empirical evidence", CEPS Working Document No. 388, Centre for European Policy Studies, Brussels, February.

Van Rompuy, H., J.M. Barroso, M. Draghi and J-C Juncker (2012), "Towards a Genuine Economic and Monetary Union" (Four Presidents Report), 26 June, Brussels.

7. RECOVERY AND RESOLUTION, THE SINGLE RESOLUTION MECHANISM AND DEPOSIT GUARANTEE SCHEMES

Among the many responses to the financial crisis, the most novel has been the insistence on specific financial sector resolution frameworks. What started out as a discussion in the early days of the financial crisis on 'living wills' segued into a discussion on bail-ins. Banks must now have detailed recovery plans readily available, and authorities are invested with the fullest powers to apply early intervention policies in the event that minimum capital requirements are not met, with the possibility of wiping out shareholders and bail-in debtors. For the Banking Union, this took the form of a new EU authority with the Single Resolution Mechanism (SRM). What has been agreed already for the banking sector is now on the table for insurance companies and market infrastructure as well. But resolution frameworks are still largely theoretical, and only a real crisis within a major financial institution, infrastructure or region will be able to test whether they work effectively.

Similar bail-in proposals have been developed at international level. The global systemically important European banks will also become subject to the total loss absorbency capacity (TLAC) requirement, designed by the Financial Stability Board (FSB), which seems compatible but nevertheless contains important differences with the EU's minimum requirement for own funds and eligible liabilities (MREL).

This chapter analyses the main elements of the new EU bank resolution requirements, the powers of the resolution authorities and the single authority for the SSM, and the role of deposit protection schemes.

7.1 Resolution: BRRD, SRM and state aid

The agreements on the bank recovery and resolution Directive (BRRD) and the Single Resolution Mechanism (SRM), the second pillar of the Banking Union, were milestones. One of the key objectives is to ensure that insolvent banks can be resolved in an orderly and uniform manner in the EU without state aid. A single resolution board plays a key role in ensuring that this process unfolds under a unique governance structure, at least for the eurozone. A single bank resolution fund should function as the backstop in the Banking Union, breaking the link between the funding costs of the bank and the sovereign. None of this structure was in place when the financial crisis hit: no member state had a separate bank resolution authority nor were there resolution funds or a European structure to coordinate bail-outs, apart from the EU's state aid control authority. Combined with the mandatory bail-in and pre-funded deposit guarantee schemes, the building blocks are now in place to deal with a crisis in banking, and bar banks from direct access to taxpayers' money.

But will there be no more state support? The SRM still allows for emergency liquidity assistance (ELA) by the national central banks and for guarantees or equity purchases by the member states, in which case state aid rules can apply. State aid rules will also apply insofar as the European Commission could impose conditions on the use of resolution funds, in line with the principles applied during the financial crisis, such as burden-sharing with other debt holders and behavioural constraints. The single resolution fund will take some time to be well-funded and its future size remains small in comparison to the size of the eurozone banking sector, but the European Stability Mechanism (ESM) can be used as the ultimate, although not unlimited, backstop (the ESM direct recapitalisation instrument) as was clarified by the Eurogroup on 10 June 2014.

Any discussion today on the backstop in Banking Union thus has to start from the new structure, although the transition period raises some questions. The SRM is applicable from 2016 onwards, but the board is operational from 2015 onwards. The BRRD should be implemented by 2015, but its provisions on bail-in only apply from 2016. Lastly, there are the EU's state aid rules, on which the Commission has published its ultimate post-crisis guidelines in July

2013. They require, until the BRRD comes into force, only bail-in of subordinated debt.

It should be recalled that harmonisation attempts of bank resolution are almost as old as the single market. Proposals have been made since the end of the 1980s to harmonise winding-up procedures of banks, in line with the home country control principle of the free provision of financial services directives. A first directive on the reorganisation and winding-up of credit institutions (Directive 2001/24/EC) was adopted in 2001 after many years of discussion. It introduced the principles of unity and universality of liquidation procedures, and required the home member state authorities of a bank to have sole jurisdiction over a bank and their decisions to be recognised in all the other member states. It establishes that the law of the home member state determines all the effects of reorganisation measures or winding-up proceedings. The degree of harmonisation was minimal, supervisory practices too divergent, and the principles of information sharing between home and host left much to be desired. In the few cases of bank failures that occurred for banks with EU-wide operations after the collapse of Lehman Brothers, such as the Icelandic banks or Fortis, host-country rules were applied, meaning that host-country authorities took over the operations of a foreign bank. A much more far-reaching harmonisation was thus needed, which the BRRD and SRM undertake.

This part reviews the main principles introduced by the BRRD and the SRM and analyses the interaction with the EU's competition policy rules. It addresses the question of how bank recovery and resolution will function from now on in the EU, and what questions remain to be resolved.

7.2   The BRRD's ambit

The degree of harmonisation of the BRRD is far-reaching and addresses in detail the planning of recovery and resolution by banks and resolution authorities, the need for early intervention, the bail-in of senior debt holders and other resolution tools, and the creation of a resolution fund. Even if the BRRD is a directive, it is far-reaching, in a field where before national laws were unclear in the powers for authorities. It is a major step forward and can be expected to influence the rules beyond the banking industry.

The focal point of the BRRD is the minimum of 8% contractual bail-in instruments as a share of total liabilities (Art. 44), which applies from 2016 onwards. When losses affect the minimum capital base, common equity tier 1 items are reduced in proportion to the losses, and additional tier 1, tier 2 and certain subordinated instruments are converted into capital. When this is not sufficient, senior liabilities will be written down, in a way that respects the *pari passu* treatment of creditors and the statutory ranking of claims under the applicable insolvency law (Recital 77). An independent valuation of the assets and liabilities of the institution will therefore be undertaken before taking resolution action or exercising the power to write down or convert relevant capital instruments (Art. 36). This valuation will "not assume any potential future provision of extraordinary public financial support or central bank emergency liquidity assistance or any central bank liquidity assistance provided under non-standard collateralization" (Art. 37.5).

A bail-in requires that banks' balance sheets have sufficient liabilities that can be bailed in, in a progressive and hierarchical manner. The bail-in can apply to all liabilities, with the exception of covered deposits, covered bonds and other collateralised instruments, short-term liabilities, and liabilities related to fiduciary functions on the bank (Art. 44). Resolution authorities will require a minimum requirement for own funds and eligible liabilities (MREL) for bail-in, to be met at all times. For groups, the minimum requirement is set by the group-level resolution authority, decided upon in cooperation with host countries, with the EBA mediating if no decision has been reached between national authorities (Art. 45.9). A proposal shall be made on a harmonised application of the MREL by the EU Commission before the end of 2016, on the basis of an EBA report (Art. 45).

The bail-in is only part of a broader series of options to resolve a bank, which are also set out in the Directive. It starts with early intervention, the removal of management or the appointment of a temporary administrator (Art. 35). Other specific tools discussed include the bridge institution tool, the sale of business tool and the asset separation ('bad bank') tool (Arts 37-42). In each of the cases, the authorities are vested with appropriate powers to undertake these actions, "without obtaining the consent of the shareholders of the institutions under resolution or any third party other than the bridge institution, and without complying with any procedural requirements under company or securities law" (Art. 42.1). "When applying the resolution tools and exercising the resolution powers, Member States shall ensure that they comply with the Union State aid framework, where applicable" (Art. 34.3).

If these actions are not sufficient, resolution authorities may make a contribution to the institution under resolution to cover losses or shore up the capital (Art. 44.4). But this can only be done after the 8% bail-in threshold is reached, to an amount not exceeding 5% of a bank's liabilities, and in full respect of EU state aid rules. Member states can also provide extraordinary public financial support through additional financial stabilisation tools, such as equity support and temporary public ownership, but again as a last resort, after all other measures have been exploited, and following state aid rules (Arts 56-58).

A second focal point of the Directive is the requirement to designate resolution authorities with all the powers necessary to apply the resolution tools described above to institutions and to entities (Arts 62-65). This includes the power to take control of an institution under resolution and exercise all the rights and powers conferred upon the shareholders. For banking groups, resolution colleges will be created, with the group consolidating supervisor in the lead. This may include the implementation of a group resolution scheme, in case all authorities involved agree (Art. 91). But the challenges for the group administrator will be great, as the resolution authorities of the host member state can object to the decisions of the group-level resolution authority, "not only on appropriateness of resolution actions and measures but also on ground of the need to protect financial stability in that Member State" (Recital 97). "The resolution college should not be a decision-making body, but a platform facilitating decision-making by national authorities. The joint decisions should be taken by the national authorities concerned" (Recital 98).

The objectives of resolution are to ensure the continuity of critical functions, preserve financial stability and "to protect public funds by minimising reliance on extraordinary public financial support" (Art. 31). The resolution authorities intervene if the determination that the institution is failing or is likely to fail has been made by the competent authority. This implies that supervisory and resolution authorities should cooperate closely, and that they can intervene even before a licence has been withdrawn. State support is still possible to keep an institution afloat "in order to remedy a serious disturbance in the economy of a Member State and preserve financial stability" (Art. 32.4d). This "shall be confined to solvent institutions and shall be conditional on final approval under the Union State aid framework. Those measures shall be of a precautionary and temporary nature and shall be proportionate to remedy the consequences of the serious disturbance and shall not be used to offset losses that the institution has incurred or is likely to incur in the near future." Such support measures "shall be limited to injections necessary to address capital shortfall established in the national, Union or SSM-wide stress tests, asset quality reviews or equivalent exercises conducted by the European Central Bank, EBA or national authorities" (Art. 32.4d, Art. 16.3d in SRM). These provisions will be reviewed by the Commission by 31 December 2015.

A third key element of the Directive is the establishment of a resolution fund, financed by bank contributions. By 31 December 2024, the fund should reach at least 1% of the amount of covered deposits of all the locally authorised institutions, with the possibility to set target levels in excess of that amount. To deal with the resolution of groups, the funds should have the power to lend from other funds in the EU, or to mutualise the national funds. The fund can only be used to resolve a bank and to contribute to a bank under resolution only after the 8% was bailed-in, and the resolution financing arrangement may not exceed 5% of the total liabilities (Art. 44.5). State aid rules apply when the resolution fund comes in.

A difficult issue in an EU context is how to balance the existence of two different resolution strategies: single point of entry (SPOE) and the multiple point of entry (MPOE) approaches. In SPOE, the home authority applies resolution powers at the top parent company level, ideally the holding company, through the absorption of losses by the parent. In MPOE, resolution powers may be applied differently to different parts of the group, and is more adapted to banks with separately capitalised subsidiaries. MPOE nevertheless requires actions to be coordinated across jurisdictions so as to avoid conflicts or inconsistencies that undermine the effectiveness of separate resolution actions.

The BRRD describes in detail how groups may provide financial support to any other party to the agreement that meets the conditions for early intervention, without it being a prerequisite (Art. 19). MPOE may, however, lead to disagreements among supervisory authorities on the approach to take to a bank in trouble, with the EBA performing the task of mediator (Art. 20). This problem should be lifted by the existence of the Single Resolution Mechanism (SRM), at least for the SSM, although it will remain a challenge for the new single resolution board to align different countries, and different banks. The operational structure as created by the BRRD remains loose and could lead to ring-fencing in case of trouble and strengthen the tendency towards subsidiarisation, which could further reduce financial integration in the EU and affect financial sector efficiency.

7.3   A Single Resolution Mechanism for the SSM

The SRM regulation creates a centralised but complex system of decision-making for bank resolution in the eurozone, and for the countries participating in the SSM. Through the intergovernmental agreement, it will be endowed with adequate financing means through the establishment of a fund with a target level of 1% of covered deposits, or approximately €55 billion based on European Commission estimates. This fund should start to irrevocably mutualise national funds by 2016, with 40% of the available means within the national compartments in the first year and 60% in the second year, and equal amounts in the subsequent six years up to 2024, until it is fully mutualised. The agreement was signed by 26 member states on 21 May 2014 (all except Sweden and the UK).

The centralised decision-making structure is composed of one board, which can meet in an executive and a plenary session. The board exercises the tasks or powers, which, according to the BRRD, are in the hands of the national resolution authorities (Art. 5). It is composed in its executive session of a chair, vice chair·and four other members, and was established from 2015 onwards, in Brussels. The ECB and the European Commission have representatives on the board. It is accountable to the plenary session of all national resolution authorities, to the European Parliament and the participating national member states. It is independent and has its own budget, separate from the EU budget, funded by contributions from national resolution authorities. Created under EU law, however, it functions as an agency of the European Commission, and will be political.

The Single Resolution Board (SRB) is tasked with drawing-up resolution plans for the significant banks within the SSM in cooperation with the national authorities and setting the minimum requirement for own funds and eligible liabilities. Non-significant banks continue to fall under the responsibility of the national resolution authorities, under the control of the SRB. In case of crisis, the SRB shall decide on the adoption of a resolution scheme, in cooperation with the Commission and the EU Council. The complexity of the decision-making in the SRM came in for heavy criticism during the debates on the draft, raising questions whether it would ever work. The moment the SSM declares a bank is failing or likely to fail, the SRM's board must adopt a resolution plan. The decision on this plan is adopted by the SRM board, in which delegates from the national resolution authorities where the bank is active also participate. It decides with a simple majority, each delegate having one vote. The Commission has 24 hours to object to the plan, or it can ask the Council within 12 hours whether it objects to the plan (Art. 18).

The complexity of the SRM is aggravated by the fact that the EBA also needs to make an assessment of recovery plans of banking groups (see also EBA, 2014). Hence the likelihood of overlaps between the EBA and the ECB for supervision also exists between the EBA and the SRM for resolution.

Another issue of debate were the contributions by a bank to the fund, which should be calculated pro rata to the amount of its liabilities (excluding own funds and covered deposits) with respect to the aggregate liabilities (excluding own funds and covered deposits) of all the institutions authorised in the participating member states. Contributions will be adjusted in proportion to the risk profile of each institution. The fund was agreed as an intergovernmental agreement "to provide maximum legal certainty", and comes into force once it has been ratified by 90% of the weighted votes of signatories.

The SRM makes extensive reference to the state aid framework. All aid, including aid from the single resolution fund, must be compatible with the EU's state aid framework. *Prima facie,*

SRF financing would not qualify as state aid since it is decided at EU level by the SRB, not by member state authorities, and the SRF funds are managed by the SRB. However, in the course of the negotiations, non-SSM participating member states argued that there is a potential threat that the SRF financing could be used in a manner that could favour the participating member state's banks, and distort competition (Zavvos & Kaltsouni, 2014). The SRM allows the EU Commission to check the compatibility of use of the SRF with the single market (Art. 19), and thus gives it a second level control over the SRB, apart from the control over a resolution plan.

The SRB cannot engage the member states. The SRM regulation states that "decisions or actions of the Board, the Commission or the Council shall neither require Member States to provide extraordinary public financial support nor impinge on the budgetary sovereignty and fiscal responsibilities of the Member States" (Art. 6). Member states can still provide aid "to remedy a serious disturbance in the economy of a Member State and preserve financial stability", which refers to Art. 107.3b of the Treaty, which was also invoked during the crisis (see chapter 8 on state aid). This can be composed of guarantees or capital support. The latter should "be limited to injections necessary to address capital shortfalls established in the national, Union or SSM-wide stress tests, asset quality reviews or equivalent exercises conducted by the ECB, EBA or national authorities, where applicable, confirmed by the competent authority" (Art. 16.3). But they "shall be conditional on final approval under State aid rules" (Art. 16.3).

The same applies in case the European Stability Mechanism (ESM) is used as a direct bank recapitalisation instrument. This instrument, as clarified by the Eurogroup on 10 June 2014, may be activated in case a bank fails to attract sufficient capital from private sources, and the ESM member is unable to recapitalise. "A bail-in of 8% of all liabilities will be a precondition for using the instrument, as well as the resources available in the ESM members' national resolution funds." The aid will be provided in accordance with EU state aid rules. The facility has a recapitalisation capacity of €60 billion.

7.4 Interaction with the state aid framework

The new rules on resolution tie in with the approach of the European Commission's competition authority (DG Comp), which published its ultimate guidelines in a July 2013 Communication (see chapter 8 in this book). They replace and complement previous communications that were published during the financial crisis. The Communication clearly establishes that financial stability remains the overarching objective for the Commission in reacting to a financial crisis, "whilst ensuring that State aid and distortions of competition between banks and across Member States are kept to the minimum". The rules reiterate that state aid can only be accepted after hybrid capital and subordinated debt holders have contributed to reducing the capital shortfall "to the maximum extent" (Art. 41 Communication). But the Commission does "not require a contribution from senior debt holders (in particular from insured deposits, uninsured deposits, bonds and all other senior debt) as a mandatory component" (Art. 42), which is the big difference in the BRRD framework. The Communication repeats that future state recapitalisation measures can only be accepted on very strict conditions, once other means, such as bail-ins, have been exhausted, and after a restructuring plan has been accepted by the Commission (Arts 29-30). Only in exceptional circumstances, when financial stability is at risk, can measures be accepted ex post (Arts 45-51), which does not prevent the compliance with burden-sharing measures. Guarantees and liquidity support can be granted before a restructuring plan is approved, but only after notification and temporary approval, following the conditions set in the previous communications, including adequate remuneration, and behavioural restrictions. They are restricted to banks that have no capital shortfall (Items 56-58).

These rules, together with the elements of the new broader resolution framework, were applied to the Banco Espirito Santo (BES) case (August 2014), whereby the state capital injection of €4.9 billion to the Bridge Bank was authorised by the European Commission. It noted that the full contribution of shareholders and of subordinated debt holders to the losses of BES was ensured, but that EU state aid rules did not require any contribution from depositors or other senior debt holders.

The July 2013 Communication also reiterated the conditions for emergency liquidity assistance (ELA) by the central bank and support by the deposit guarantee scheme. ELA needs to be fully secured by collateral, with haircuts and at penalising rates. State guarantees on ELA will be considered state aid, and the use of deposit guarantee funds, in case they are used for restructuring purposes, may constitute state aid and will be assessed by the Commission (Items 62-63). Also, the ECB restated its policy with regard to ELA in October 2013, noting that it is limited "to a solvent financial institution, or group of solvent financial institutions, that is facing temporary liquidity problems, without such operation being part of the single monetary policy. Responsibility for the provision of ELA lies with the NCBs (national central banks) concerned. This means that any costs of, and the risks arising from, the provision of ELA are incurred by the relevant NCB." But NCBs should inform the ECB of the details of any ELA operation daily, and should obtain ex ante approval for any operation exceeding a threshold of €500 million. This policy was applied to Greek banks in 2015, when the ECB authorised ELA by the Greek central bank to face the situation of large deposit withdrawals in the Greek banking system, although there were strong doubts about their solvency.

7.5 More harmony in deposit guarantee schemes

The agreement reached in early 2014 on a further harmonisation of deposit guarantee schemes is often overlooked in the policy debates. It is indeed the case that no single deposit guarantee system was created, as was set out in the Four Presidents Report,[55] but an agreement was reached on a far-reaching harmonisation and update of the previous directives containing rules on pre-funding, the maximum pay-out deadlines and the functioning across borders. Again, none of this existed before, even considering the limited changes that were agreed upon in the early days of the financial crisis.

Deposit guarantee schemes are an important building block for financial stability. By ensuring a generous level of protection, depositors should be motivated to entrust their money to banks and not to make a run on their bank. This assumes, however, that

---

[55] Van Rompuy et al. (2012).

depositor protection schemes have the necessary funds available, and that they can be paid out rapidly, upon failure of the bank. The EU's 1994 Directive undertook only a very limited form of harmonisation, i.e. it made a minimum level of €20,000 coverage obligatory in the EU, but did not allow for competition between schemes, i.e. branches of host-country banks were not allowed to export more generous levels of protection, whereas branches of banks with home countries with lower levels of protection were allowed to top-up to the level of the host country. The failure of the Directive was clear with the start of the financial crisis, as in most cases states chose to bail out banks rather than liquidate them and let the deposit protection system bail out depositors. Hence the radical increase of the level of coverage to a maximum of €50,000 in October 2008 (and later €100,000) was intended to maintain financial stability.

How necessary a common deposit guarantee scheme is for the Banking Union remains debatable. Given the premise of the Banking Union, breaking the vicious circle between the sovereigns and the banks, a common system should be an important element. Maintaining different contribution levels and forms of financing would maintain the vicious circle. However, the level of funds kept in all EU deposit insurance systems today remains very limited, and totals about €18.6 billion (2011), less than one-half the level that will be needed when the new directive is fully implemented. In addition, only scant funds were effectively used during the crisis, in most cases; the state intervened directly to support banks. Hence other elements probably matter much more.

The degree of harmonisation achieved by the 2014 recast of the 1994 Directive is an important step forward. Although it does not introduce a single fund, it goes far enough to make deposit insurance systems a more important building block for financial stability in the EU and the EEA, at least over time. It establishes that within 10 years of this Directive's publication, i.e. by July 2024, the available financial means of a DGS shall at least reach a target level of 0.8% of the amount of the covered deposits of its members (Art. 10). In the event that bank deposits are declared unavailable, schemes need to cover up to €100,000 or the equivalent within seven working days (from 2024, 10 to 15 days during the transition), at a ratio of one depositor per credit institution. In case the fund is not sufficient, it can call upon *ex-post* contributions (of 0.5% of the covered deposits), or it can borrow from the government or the market.

As a step towards a common EU-wide fund, the Commission had introduced borrowing between funds, which proved to be a 'hot potato' during the discussions. The Directive allows for borrowing between funds, but on a voluntary basis, not exceeding 0.5% of covered deposits of the borrowing DGS, and subject to repayment within five years. For another problem, the treatment of deposits with branches, the text leaves this as the financial responsibility of the home member state of the bank, but the pay-out will take place through the DGS in the host member state, acting as a 'single point of contact' on behalf of the DGS in the home member state (Art. 14). For branches of third-country credit institutions, they must join a DGS in operation in a member state.

The level of protection, €100,000, is seen to be very high, especially for certain new member states, and is applied per depositor per bank (which may be individuals or enterprises). Hence the incentives for depositors to monitor the riskiness of the limited banks could be seen to contribute to moral hazard. The Directive, however, allows DGS to use their own risk-based methods for determining and calculating the contributions by their members, taking due account of the risk profiles of the various business models, with the EBA proposing non-binding guidelines on technical aspects (Art. 13).

The DGS Directive leaves an important backdoor open to the sovereign-bank nexus, i.e. it does not cover "contractual schemes" or "institutional protection schemes" that are not officially recognised as DGS (Art. 1.3). This means that member states with additional generous protection schemes can decide to exclude them from the scope of the Directive, thus leaving an important distortion to the single market.

Hence, within the SSM, depositor protection will remain decentralised, unlike the supervision of the significant banks and resolution. Considering that consumer protection remains a host-country responsibility in the SSM and the EU, this does not seem problematic, as the EU managed to agree on further harmonisation of the funding and functioning of depositor protection schemes. The crucial issue will be the link with resolution, and ensuring that resolution actions, particularly a call to the deposit insurance fund, are closely coordinated across the member states. It is not unimaginable under the current structure that reactions to a cross-border banking crisis will in practice unwind differently across the EU, even more so with a decentralised deposit insurance fund. The DGS Directive allows member states to use its funds for resolution, in the last instance to prevent a bank failure, and when certain conditions are met. But could this be decided over a weekend, and will different member states take the same decision for their DGS? Under the BRRD, member states can still decide differently for a cross-border bank according to their financial stability concerns. This is less likely within the SSM with the SRM, although it remains possible that the SRM board will not agree.

7.6 Conclusions

The new resolution framework is clear. All extraordinary public support for a bank that does not meet the required capital levels is subject to state aid rules, and can only come in after burden-sharing and bail-in rules have been applied. The difference between the current and the new rules is that bail-in can under the BRRD and SRM be extended to the senior debt holders, including depositors, above €100,000. It is only in exceptional circumstances, i.e. a serious disturbance in a national economy, that exceptions can be accepted.

Experience is limited with bail-ins in the financial sector, and it was only applied on a large scale very late in the financial crisis, most importantly in the resolution of some Spanish savings banks in November 2012, but also in Cyprus in 2013, and more recently in particular cases in Slovenia, the Netherlands and Portugal. The question also arises how the new rules will be applied for cross-border banks that operate in several jurisdictions and under different models, and whether they would give rise to legal challenges.

Following the EU rules on the subject, the ECB (and the NCAs) will for the time being only use one prudential measure to assess a bank's soundness, i.e. Common Equity Tier 1 (CET1)), as it did in the AQR, which gives banks and supervisors some room for manoeuvre in the short term. CET1 is a risk-weighted capital standard, which allows for zero risk-weighting for government bonds and reduced weighting for property loans, or applies internal models for risk measurement, which for large European banks gives a low level of risk-weighted assets to total assets (see chapter 5 in this volume). In addition, the ECB has other tools at its disposal to address temporary liquidity problems in the banking sector, as it did in 2012 with the long-term refinancing operation (LTRO), and with the measures it announced again in June 2014. By 2016, however, a harmonised definition of MREL should be in place, by which time it may become a more important benchmark than CET1. But how it will be applied in practice remains to be seen.

The consistent implementation of the new resolution framework will require hard work by supervisory and resolution authorities, and by financial institutions. Many member states still have to create an authority and set up a resolution fund. Banks will need to examine their balance sheets, check the amount of debt subject to bail-in and draft recovery plans. At EU level, a new element in the supervisory structure emerged, with a single resolution authority for the SSM and later possibly for almost the entire EU, with the exception of two member states.

References

Bates, C. and S. Gleeson (2011), "Legal Aspects of Bank Bail-Ins", Client Briefing, Clifford Chance, May.

Huertas, T. (2014), *Safe to Fail: How Resolution Will Revolutionise Banking*, Basingstoke: Palgrave Macmillan.

IMF (2014), "Cross-border bank resolution: Recent developments", Board Paper, Washington, D.C., June.

Micossi, S., G. Bruzzone and M. Cassella (2014), "Bail-in Provisions in State Aid and Resolution Procedures: Are they consistent with systemic stability?", CEPS Policy Brief, Centre for European Policy Studies, Brussels.

Van Rompuy, H., J.M. Barroso, M. Draghi and J-C Juncker (2012), "Towards a Genuine Economic and Monetary Union" (Four Presidents Report), 26 June, Brussels.

Zavvos, G. and S. Kaltsouni (2014), "The Single Resolution Mechanism in the European Banking Union: Legal Foundation, Governance Structure and Financing", 15 September, available on the Social Science Research Network.

8. THE EU'S BANK STATE AID POLICY DURING THE CRISIS*

The financial crisis posed an enormous challenge for the EU's state aid regime. Conceived to ensure a level playing field in the single market, the scheme also had to show that it could be adapted to very exceptional circumstances, in the absence of an EU-wide recovery and resolution framework for systemic financial institutions. The size and nature of the aid, the number of the schemes and the complexity of the cases that had to be examined and approved were overwhelming. Although some high-profile cases of bank state aid had been dealt with by the European Commission in the past, never in the EU's half-century of history had the European Commission dealt with so many cases in such a short period of time. The approach followed during this period will thus continue to influence policy-making for a long time to come.

Throughout the crisis, 21 national schemes of state aid to the financial sector and over 90 cases of individual banks and other financial intermediaries were dealt with by the European Commission. At the height of the crisis, the effectively committed value of aid amounted to some 14.3% of the GDP of the EU. The final amount may turn out to be lower, however, as the largest part of aid was granted in remunerated guarantees of bank liabilities, which cease with the withdrawal of the guarantee, and provide income to the state. But many guarantees lasted much longer than expected at the outbreak of the crisis.

During the crisis, the EU Commission gave guidance to the private sector about its policy in applying state aid rules to the

* This chapter is drawn from Lannoo et al. (2010), *Bank state aid in the financial crisis: Fragmentation or level playing field*, CEPS Task Force Report and was updated up to February 2015, taking into account the period of the sovereign debt crisis. Valuable research assistance by Willem Pieter De Groen is gratefully acknowledged.

financial sector. The EU published eight Communications, but it remains an open question how closely this policy was applied in practice. Considering the approach taken in specific state aid cases, it seems that the policy followed was more ad hoc. Some general principles were followed, including new conditions that had not been applied before, but it seems that the end-result, certainly at European level, was a more uneven playing field. Some member states' banks were in better shape when the crisis hit, but some states were also better prepared to respond to the crisis and to make their state aid schemes compatible with EU rules. Different forms of restructuring packages were thus not necessarily only institution-specific, but also country-specific.

The legal provisions of the EU framework to assess state aid are unique. The EU is the only international entity with real powers to assess aid and its distortions to competition and trade, and to enforce remedies, but its framework is limited to aid given by EU member states. Beyond that, the EU needs to rely on international agreements, most importantly the WTO's GATS, which are much weaker than what exists in the EU, and without any case law so far.

8.1 The EU's state aid policy: Rationale and perspective

State aid control is a core EU task, enshrined in the Treaty from its founding. Its objective is to ensure that government interventions do not distort competition and trade in the internal market. State aid is defined as 'any aid granted by a Member State or through State resources in any form whatsoever which distorts or threatens to distort competition' (Art. 107 TFEU). Subsidies granted to individuals or general measures open to all enterprises are not covered by Art. 107 and do not constitute state aid.

The EU Treaty pronounces a general prohibition of state aid. In some circumstances, however, government interventions can be permitted. These concern measures to promote regional development, responses to serious economic disturbances, and aid to economic sectors in trouble. The European Commission has the sole competence to decide when state aid can be permitted. The Treaty provides that all new aid measures must be notified and approved by the European Commission prior to their implementation, if not, the aid is invalid. It is only after the approval by the Commission that an aid measure can be implemented. Incompatible state aid can be recovered. The Commission can be overruled by the EU Council of Ministers, which can decide, acting unanimously, that aid is compatible with the single market, in derogation from the provisions of Art. 107.

Until the crisis hit, the experience of applying state aid rules to the financial sector was limited to a few, but high profile cases. The most well-known ones are the Crédit Lyonnais case and the German regional banks ruling. In the former case, the European Commission decided in 1995 that Crédit Lyonnais, in return for the green light on the €6.9 billion (FF45 billion) in state aid, had to reduce its commercial operations abroad, including a substantial part of its European banking network, by at least 35% by the end of 1998.[56] In the Landesbank case, the European Commission agreed with the German government in 2001 and 2002 to abolish the system of state guarantees for the regional savings banks (Landesbanken) and distinguish between the public policy and purely commercial tasks of these institutions. The continued use of state guarantees was allowed for public policy tasks, e.g. the financing of SMEs and infrastructure, housing, investments for environmental protection and cooperation with developing countries.[57]

Some have argued before that the EU's state aid rules are not entirely appropriate for the banking sector, because of its special nature (Grande, 1999). Public subsidies may be needed in the banking sector in prolongation of the objectives pursued by regulation and supervision, and may not necessarily distort competition, as the entire financial system benefits from stability. When combating systemic risk, state aid is used to prevent a serious disruption of the financial system, and of the overall economy. In addition, the aid may be granted through special liquidity support by the central bank. Hence the overall public interest is at stake, not simply a private one. This public interest is essentially monitored by national supervisory authorities and central banks, implying that the control of state aid, when related to financial supervisory and systemic stability issues, should be in their hands.

---

[56] European Commission, 95/547/EC of 26.07.1995.

[57] European Commission, Decisions of 17 July 2001 and 1 March 2002.

Figure 11. Non-crisis related state aid excluding railways, 1992-2013 (% of EU GDP)

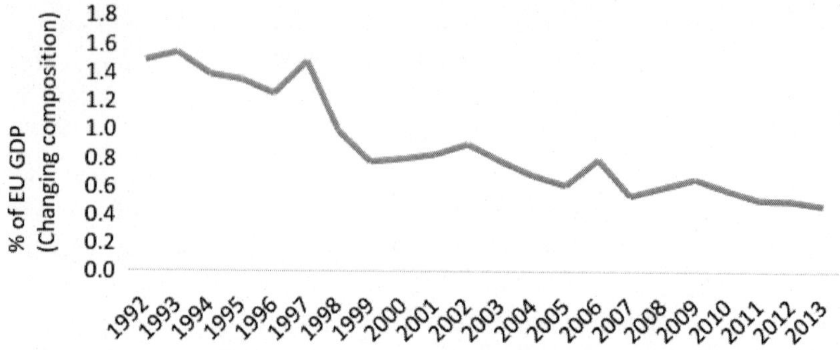

Source: Author's calculations based on EU State Aid Scoreboard 2014.

The outbreak of the financial crisis forced policy-makers to come to terms with a calamity, of proportions no one had imagined before, and to which they had to respond rapidly. Some preparations had been made before to simulate crisis, but no overall crisis framework existed. For comparison, the overall level of state aid granted in the EU between 1992 and 2007, expressed as a percentage of GDP, decreased from 1.5% per year in 1992 to 0.5% in 2007, see also Figure 11.

This chapter reviews the forms of aid that were given to the financial sector and the application of the EU's state aid policy during the financial and sovereign crisis. It demonstrates that there are vast differences in the way member states have offered and implemented aid to the financial sector, and that these differing policies have called the coherence of the single market into question. We also examine state aid in the global context, and question whether existing international tools for ensuring a level playing field are sufficient, given the global nature of the financial industry.

8.2 Financial sector support during the financial and sovereign crisis

The EU's state aid policy for the financial sector was not challenged during the first year of the financial crisis (August 2007-August 2008). It is only in the aftermath of the collapse of Lehman Brothers, and after a special Eurogroup, meeting at the level of heads of state and government in the Elysée Palace in Paris on 12th October 2008, that its application was temporarily relaxed to deal with the extraordinary circumstances in financial markets. Political leaders did however not realise that the temporary nature of these measures would last much longer than they expected, some of which are still in place at the day of writing, March 2015.

In absence of a European-wide bail-out plan, the Eurogroup took two decisions on 12 October 2008:

-   Governments can provide state guarantees to bank debt issues for up to five years under well-determined conditions, and can participate in these issues. All banks should be eligible for these operations, including foreign-owned banks.
-   Governments can take equity stakes in financial institutions and recapitalise banks in trouble.

The Eurogroup requested that governments avoid national measures that would negatively affect the functioning of the internal market and harm other member states. The Eurogroup committed to "coordinate in providing these guarantees, as significant differences in national implementation could have a counter-productive effect, creating distortions in banking markets". The support actions would be "designed in order to avoid any distortion in the level playing field and possible abuse at the expense of the non-beneficiaries of these arrangements".[58]

The Eurogroup suggested to the European Central Bank to fulfil its role in assuring sufficient liquidity for the financial sector and to react with flexibility to market circumstances. In particular, the ECB was asked to ease its rules on assets eligible as collateral in liquidity providing operations, on which the central bank acted a few days later. From that moment on, the ECB dramatically expanded the eligibility criteria of marketable and non-marketable assets, including the lowering of the credit threshold for these assets from an A- to a BBB- credit assessment by an eligible External Credit Assessment Institution (ECAI) or rating agent.[59] Later during the sovereign crisis, the ECB decided to temporarily accept credit claims, such as enterprise loans, as collateral and to suspend the

---

[58] Eurogroup meeting, 12 October 2008, pp. 2-3.

[59] ECB, Measures to further expand the collateral framework, Press release, 15 October 2008.

application of the minimum credit rating threshold in the collateral eligibility requirements for debt instruments issued by the central government of countries that are under an EU-IMF programme.[60]

The Eurogroup decisions were later endorsed by the Autumn European Council (October 2008), which broadened their application to the EU as a whole. The European Council endorsed a flexible interpretation of the EU's state aid rules, given the exceptional circumstances.[61] EU leaders allowed exceptional bank state aid so as to restore financial stability and to allow credit flows to continue.

Hence, to have a correct picture of 'state' support during the crisis, the different actions must be seen in combination. Enhanced credit support by the ECB and quantitative easing by the Bank of England are not state aid, but help to stabilise the financial system. The full list of financial sector stabilisation measures comprises:

- Government financial sector stabilisation measures:
  - (Re)capitalisation
  - Asset relief interventions:
    - o support for impaired assets in asset support programmes
    - o 'bad bank' schemes
  - Guarantees:
    - o bank deposits
    - o interbank lending
    - o bank bonds
  - Other liquidity support measures:
    - o participation in debt issues/loans
    - o underwriting of subordinated debt
- Central bank monetary policy adjustments and liquidity support
  - Lowering of rates for main refinancing operations and standing facilities, fine-tuning operations and longer term credit provision (LTRO)
  - Enhanced credit support, composed of full allotment in liquidity providing operations, expansion of eligible

---

[60] ECB, Measures to preserve collateral availability, 8 December 2011 and 6 September 2012 respectively.

[61] European Council, 15-16 October 2008, p. 2.

collateral and direct purchases of securities (quantitative easing)

Figure 12 below shows that the policy was successful for the eurozone. The large spread between the 3-month Euribor and the ECB's main refinancing rate was gradually narrowed as a result of the exceptional measures agreed upon at the Eurogroup meeting. It is thus the combination of state aid, the ECB's monetary policy and enhanced credit support that has stabilised the situation all along the financial and sovereign crisis. The 3-month Euribor stabilised at 0.7% in the last quarter of 2009, or well below the ECB main refinancing rate of 1%, which indicates that liquidity was abundant. Though only temporary, the ECB intended to start reducing the eligible collateral in credit providing operations, but the sovereign debt crisis that started in early 2010 forced it to delay this measure. Greek government paper was rated BBB- (Fitch, S&P), which would have curtailed access of Greek banks to the ECB's liquidity providing operations.

Figure 12. Evolution of the ECB's refinancing rate and 3-month Euribor (Jan 2005 - Jan 2015)

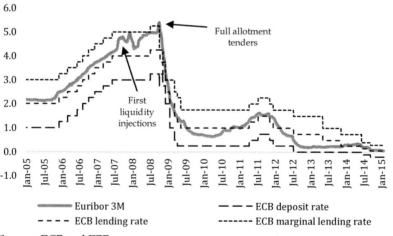

Sources: ECB and EBF.

The intervention of the ECB contrasted, at least in the initial phase, with those of other central banks, in particular with the Federal Reserve and the Bank of England, which were more active in the direct purchase of securities with the so-called 'quantitative easing' schemes. In addition, asset support and debt guarantee programmes were more extensive in the US and the UK than in the eurozone, in the sense that initially a distinction could be made between the 'Anglo-Saxon' world and continental Europe in the response to the crisis. According to numbers released by the Bank of England, state support for the financial sector, including central bank assistance, was up to 74% of GDP in the UK, 48% in the US, compared to 28% in the eurozone until end-2009. This changed with the sovereign debt crisis of the first half of 2010.

8.3 Central banks' interaction with the financial system in times of crisis

Central banks can thus support the financial system through the conditions of the liquidity-providing operations. In normal circumstances, central banks control money supply through the central interest rate on credit for the banking sector. Banks can access liquidity in exchange for collateral, which is limited to high-quality securities, on which a haircut is applied. The ECB for example applies a fixed valuation haircut of up to 5.5% on highly-rated 10-year government bonds (declining with maturity), or up to 16% for top quality asset backed securities. To cope with market fluctuations, margin calls are applied by the ECB.

During the financial crisis, the ECB initially lowered its conditions for acceptable collateral from A- to BBB-, without changing the valuation haircuts. It later scrapped the minimum credit rating threshold altogether for Greece, Ireland, Portugal, the 'Programme countries', and later for Cyprus, and subject to special haircuts. This implies that securities may well have been accepted by the central bank with valuation haircuts that were above the market price at a given moment, allowing banks to arbitrage. It is unclear whether the margin calls have been fully applied in the volatile financial market context of the period 2010-2012, or whether they have been fully applied for less marketable financial instruments.

In its most extreme form, central banks can buy assets directly in the markets at distressed prices to inject liquidity and bring stability into the financial system ('quantitative easing'), as was widely carried out in the UK and the US. These operations artificially shore up the value of the assets, and are a support to the financial system. Quantitative easing, however, is risky and may affect the capital base of the central banks, if losses have to be taken on these purchases.

The EMU form of extensive liquidity assistance were the long-term refinancing operations (LTROs), by which the ECB injected more than €1 trillion over two to three years, the first on 10 December 2011 with €489 billion, the second on 19 February 2012 with €530 billion, in the European banking markets. Banks in trouble mostly in southern European member states, were large participants, but also banks based outside the eurozone, but with subsidiaries within, participated. According to the Financial Times, based upon Morgan Stanley data, Bankia, the former Caja Madrid savings bank, got the lion's share with €40 billion, followed by Intesa Sanpaolo with €36 billion, Dexia with €32.5 billion, Unicredit with €23.5 billion, BBVA with €22 billion and Lloyds Banking Group with €13 billion.[62] The ECB's action thus provided relief outside the eurozone as well.

Within EMU, direct aid by central banks to the financial system is forbidden under the Treaty. However, as financial stability remains, even under Banking Union, a national responsibility, national central banks can still provide emergency liquidity assistance (ELA). This is also 'state aid' and needs to be authorised by the EU Commission. Also the agreement of the ECB's Governing Council is required for ELA. In the case of Fortis, for example, the Belgian central bank (NBB) gave emergency liquidity assistance of €60 billion, which had to be specifically authorised by the ECB. This also happened later for Dexia Bank.

8.4   Types of direct bank state aid

State aid to the financial sector can be offered in four main forms, as described below.

First, states can provide *capital* support to strengthen the capital base of financial institutions. In recapitalisation programmes, governments inject funds into banks in exchange for direct equity, preferred shares or subordinated debt (as a form of

---

[62] *Financial Times*, 2 March 2012.

hybrid capital). In a situation of serious distress, as the financial crisis, banks may need new capital, which will be difficult or impossible due to market uncertainty. Recapitalising banks can improve the functioning and stability of the banking system and maintain financing flows to the wider economy. If the government obtains more than fifty percent of the voting rights the recapitalisation is considered to be nationalisation. Public ownership itself is not a form of state aid – the EU Treaty is neutral with regard to the form of ownership – it is the capital injection in a bank in trouble that forms state aid. In most cases, the goal of nationalisation is to return the bank to health with the objective of one day returning it to the private sector. This discussion started already in some member states as the financial situation started to normalise from 2013 onwards.

Second, a special form to absorb losses in the financial system is *asset relief*, i.e. the creation of a so-called bad bank. In a bad bank, banks get a delay to reimburse their creditors until the financial system normalises, and assets recover. Under a bad bank scheme, assets are protected or guaranteed by the state in separate legal entities. Bad banks can be private, controlled by the bank in trouble or by the banking sector at large, or they can be owned by the state. Relieving financial institutions of impaired assets can help a bank strengthen its balance sheet, re-gain access to liquidity, and reduce leverage. Bad bank schemes raise fundamental competition policy problems, however, related to determining the new book value of the impaired assets, tackling the distortions created by the schemes and justifying the scheme to taxpayers when public money is used to guarantee the bad assets of banks in trouble, as was the case in Belgium, Ireland and Spain.

Third, governments can *guarantee* bank deposits, banks bonds or all bank liabilities. As deposit guarantee schemes are designed for all retail depositors, funded by the banking sector and limited to a fixed maximum amount, they do not raise a state aid issue. To the extent that the deposit insurance fund is used to bail out an entire bank, as happened in the Banesto (1993) and Banco di Sicilia (1995) cases, the EU's state aid rules apply. Deposit protection can be extended to cover a broader set of bank liabilities so as to prevent gridlock in the financial system, as was done in Ireland in the

Eligible Liabilities Guarantee scheme.[63] Governments can also specifically guarantee certain bank loans and bonds to maintain the ability of banks to raise funds. Such guarantees should be remunerated, to maintain a level playing field with banks not subject to a scheme.

Fourth, governments can provide *other types liquidity support*. This considers for example direct loans from governments to banks. The other liquidity support measures are treated similarly by DG Competition as guarantees on bonds and loans. The liquidity measures need to be remunerated to maintain a level playing field. In turn, for governments it is in general less attractive to grant direct loans than guarantees, because the loans are included in the calculations of the official government debt figures.

8.5 EU state aid policy during the financial and sovereign crisis

Direct state aid during the financial and sovereign crisis posed a fundamental challenge for the application of the EU's competition policy rules, which had never faced a crisis of that magnitude. The remainder of this chapter discusses only direct state aid, and covers the period 2008-09 of the financial crisis, with massive state aid for North-European banks, and the period 2010-2012 of the sovereign crisis, and large cases of aid for Southern-European banks.

The announcement of the Irish Credit Institutions Financial Support scheme on 27 September 2008 was the first of a cascade of national bail-out plans, all of which raised to a greater or lesser degree single market competition policy problems. From the early days of the financial crisis in the autumn of 2007, the EU continued to apply its state aid policy, for example in the Northern Rock, IKB or Sachsen LB cases. With the start of the systemic crisis in autumn 2008, it temporarily accepted the exceptional circumstances of the crisis and let financial stability concerns precede over the strict application of the state aid rules. The EU Commission invoked Art. 107(3)(b) of the Treaty as legal basis, which exceptionally allows for aid to remedy a serious disturbance in the economy of a member state.

---

[63] See European Commission, State aid case N 254/2010 of 16.06.2010.

Table 7. Form of interventions by EU states in support of financial institutions, September 2007-August 2014

Member state	Guarantee schemes	Recapitali- sation schemes	Schemes combining several measures	Other measures, i.e. bad bank schemes	Affected financial institutions*
Austria			x		5
Belgium					5
Denmark	x	x			8
Finland	x	x			1
France	x	x			2
Germany			x	x	12
Greece			x		9
Ireland	x	x		x	8
Italy	x	x			1
Luxembourg					1
Netherlands	x				4
Portugal	x	x			7
Spain	x	x		x**	15
Sweden	x	x			1
UK	x		x		5
EU15	**10**	**8**	**4**	**3**	**84**
Bulgaria				x***	
Cyprus	x				2
Croatia					
Czech Republic					
Estonia					
Hungary			x		1
Latvia	x				3
Lithuania			x		2
Malta					
Poland	x	x		x***	
Romania					
Slovakia	x	x			
Slovenia	x	x			5
EU13	**5**	**3**	**2**	**2**	**13**
EU28	**15**	**11**	**6**	**5**	**97**

* This number counts cases during the financial crisis concerning one and the same bank or closely-linked network only once.
** In the case of Spain, this concerns an asset repurchase scheme.
*** Liquidation scheme.

Source: Compiled from European Commission, DG Comp, updated until August 2014.

Until August 2014, the European Commission had been notified of 21 state debt guarantee and 17 recapitalisation schemes, and 97 specific bank state aid cases. Some 13 of the old member states (except Belgium and Luxembourg) had a national scheme, and eight new member states (Bulgaria, Cyprus, Hungary, Latvia, Lithuania, Poland, Slovakia and Slovenia). Five EU member states had neither bank support schemes nor individual bank support cases, all of these new member states (Croatia, Czech Republic, Estonia, Malta and Romania). The national support schemes are in some cases limited to guarantees only, but can also comprise recapitalisation or bad bank schemes, as shown in Table 7. Germany and the UK had the most comprehensive national schemes, whereas Spain had the highest number of individual bank cases (15).

The total amount of support measures to the financial sector approved during the crisis added up to €5.4 trillion, 39.7% of the EU's GDP. It consists of general and ad hoc support for financial institutions, composed of debt guarantees, short-term liquidity support, equity (recapitalisation) and debt (subordinated debt) financing, and support for bad bank schemes. €1.9 trillion (14.3% of GDP) of this amount has been effectively used. State guarantees on bank liabilities represent the largest budgetary commitment among the aid instruments, with €3.7 trillion (27.5% of EU GDP) of approved measures, out of which €1.2 trillion (8.8% of GDP) have been effectively granted (see also Table 8). These guarantees were provided in national schemes, with varying legal frameworks and timelines. They differ in three general aspects:

- Amounts granted: Allowances available ranged from insignificant to unlimited (Belgium, Denmark and Ireland).

- Eligibility: Certain countries were much more restrictive with respect to which firms were eligible for guarantees. For example, Ireland made allowances available to any financial institution with a systemic relevance to the Irish economy. By contrast, the Dutch scheme was open only to those institutions defined as banks and having their corporate domicile or substantial operations in the Netherlands, and with an acceptable solvency ratio.

- Conditionality: While many schemes placed restrictions on executive pay, only some placed restrictions on balance sheet growth, and fewer made guarantees available only to "fundamentally sound institutions".

Table 8. Public interventions in the EU banking sector, 2008-13 (€ bn)

	Committed aid	Effectively used	% share	% EU 2013 GDP
	(A)	(B)	(B/A)	(B/GDP)
Re-capitalisation	781.8	448.2	57.3	3.31
Asset relief	599.8	188.2	31.4	1.39
Total re-capitalisation and asset relief	*1,381.6*	*636.4*	*46.1*	*4.70*
Guarantees	3,724.2	1,188.1*	31.9	8.78
Other liquidity support	269.0	104.9*	39.0	0.78
Total liquidity measures	*3,993.2*	*1,293.0*	*32.4*	*9.56*
Total	5,374.7	1,929.4	28.7	14.26

Note: For country specific data, see European Commission (2014). This does not include the revenues obtained by governments from these support schemes. *Calibrated using the aggregates of the highest end of year values per country. *Source*: European Commission (2015).

According to the latest Commission data, member states have received a total of €148 billion (1.1% of EU 2013 GDP) in revenue in exchange for their support to the banking sector.

During the crisis, the European Commission's Competition Directorate published several Communications to try to bring some order in the national support schemes. However, the Commission only succeeded gradually in doing this, as the crisis receded and the need to preserve the single market re-emerged as a policy priority. Issues such as non-discriminatory access or unjustified protection of shareholders were apparent but initially led to no or only limited reaction on the part of the EU. In total, the European Commission published eight Communications of a temporary nature.

The first Communication, published in October 2008, sets out the general principles to be respected, the successive ones focus on aspects of it, i.e. the required remuneration for state support, the treatment of impaired assets and the restructuring plans in the return to viability. The next two discuss the temporary prolongation and adaptation of certain elements of the previous communications.

The 2013 Banking Communication consolidates all the previous ones.

Overall, the Commission's objectives are to:

- demonstrate a capacity for an effective Community-level response to the financial crisis,
- limit negative spill-over among member states,
- protect the single market and
- minimise competitive distortions and moral hazard.

It should be recalled that many of these single market distortions and thorny competition policy problems could have been avoided if an effective EU bank resolution and crisis management framework had been in place. A first directive on the re-organisation and winding up of credit institutions (directive 2001/24/EC) was adopted in 2001, but the harmonisation was too limited and the supervisory practices too divergent.

The most important document in the context of this chapter, and the future shape of the European banking markets, is the July 2009 Communication on the return to viability. It states that the Commission will examine restructuring plans in view of:

- *A thorough diagnosis of a bank's problems.* The starting point for a viability plan with, where applicable, disclosure of impaired assets and off-balance sheet items.

- *A restructuring plan with a flexible and realistic timing.* A viability plan requires a stress test. It should demonstrate how the bank will return to viability without aid as soon as possible (maximum term is five years), giving details per business line on the re-structuring, funding, risk controls, governance. It should also analyse alternative considered options, such as sale of the bank or break-up.

- *Clear burden-sharing between the member state and beneficiaries.* The aid should be limited to the minimum necessary, which can include the sale of assets, although the Commission acknowledges that absolute thresholds cannot be set *ex ante*. Aid should be remunerated, but cannot be used to pay dividends or subordinated debt holders.

- *Measures to limit distortions of competition.* These will again be case-specific or tailor-made, as many elements have to be taken into consideration: the survival of the bank, the maintenance of the single market, the promotion of competitive markets. State aid cannot be used for acquisitions, a condition that applies for at least three years.

In applying these rules, the European Commission accepted new conditions. It accepted the recapitalisation of banks during the crisis, not only emergency loans and special guarantees. For non-financial corporations, the rule is that recapitalisation is only accepted after the restructuring. Recapitalisation is also seen as a more permanent measure than loans and guarantees, meaning that aid becomes longer-term, and thus more permanent, than the state aid rules as applied before. Finally, the Commission also accepted aid schemes, not only individual measures.

The Commission published its latest guidelines on the subject in July 2013, which replace the previous Communications. It sets that financial stability remains the overarching objective for the Commission in reacting to financial crisis, "whilst ensuring that State aid and distortions of competition between banks and across Member States are kept to the minimum". The rules state that state aid can only be accepted after hybrid capital and subordinated debt holders have contributed to reducing the capital shortfall 'to the maximum extent' (Art. 41 Communication). But the Commission does 'not require contribution from senior debt holders (in particular from insured deposits, uninsured deposits, bonds and all other senior debt) as a mandatory component' (Art. 42), which is the big difference with the framework of the new Bank Resolution and Recovery Directive (2014).

The Communication repeats that future state recapitalisation measures, whether in the context of stress test or asset quality review, can only be accepted on very strict conditions, once other means, such as bail-ins, have been exhausted, and after a restructuring plan has been accepted by the Commission (Art. 29-30). Only in exceptional circumstances, when financial stability is at risk can measures be accepted ex-post (Art. 45-51), which does not prevent the compliance with burden-sharing measures. Guarantees and liquidity support can be granted before a restructuring plan is approved, but only after notification and temporary approval, following the conditions set in the previous communications, including adequate remuneration, and behavioural restrictions.

They are restricted to banks that have no capital shortfall (items 56-58).

8.6 State aid cases during the financial crisis

The principles of the Return to Viability Communication formed the basis for the state aid decisions that the European Commission adopted from the autumn of 2009 onwards. Although some decisions had been taken before, such as with Commerzbank, the Commission aimed to indicate that the situation had returned to normal. In announcing the ING, KBC and Lloyds Decisions on 18 November 2009, former Competition Policy Commissioner Neely Kroes said: "We want to ensure that banks can be rebuilt so that they can play their role in helping Europe's economy to recover and will not be a long-term burden on Europe's taxpayers." The Commissioner added that three common principles underpin the Commission's approach to these cases: 1) presence of a long-term business model, 2) minimisation of taxpayer burdens and 3) the maintenance of the single market. The final approval of the measures was conditional upon the presentation of a restructuring plan capable of restoring the long-term viability of the bank without continued state support.

The announcement of the Commission Decisions regarding state-aided banks seemed to have taken markets by surprise, as the stocks of these banks fell considerably, depending on the scale of the restructuring plan. The share price of ING and Lloyds fell by about 30% in the week following the announcement. Markets appeared to be unaware of the Commission's powers to act on state aid, or had simply disregarded them. The Commission plan was also a signal to those banks that did not benefit from explicit government support during the crisis that the level playing field would be restored.

The agreement between the Commission and the home state of the bank in question is specific in each case. The ING announcement that it would divest all its insurance and investment management activities – and thus end its bank-insurance model – led to speculation that the Commission would impose the same conditions on other groups. In the KBC case, however, another deal was reached, including the divestment of the group's private banking and private equity business, and the sale of non-core activities in Central and Eastern Europe. In the case of Lloyds, probably one of the most difficult cases after the takeover of the bankrupt HBOS, the Commission took comfort from the sale of a part of the retail banking group.

The Commission applied the following criteria in judging each case:

- The aid must be limited to the *minimum necessary* to achieve the objective.
- It must be *proportional* to the contribution made by private share- and bondholders. Hence, constraints are imposed on management and owners.
- The aid must be *appropriate* and *well-targeted*.
- The aid must be *remunerated*.

Applying these criteria in practice is difficult, however. What is the strictest minimum for aid? What is proportional? What conditions can be imposed on state-aided banks? As Table 9 and Box 3 below demonstrate, the European Commission has clearly applied certain principles consistently: adequate remuneration, dividend ban, price leadership ban, but the degree of downsizing and the core market reduction differs importantly.

Table 9. Comparing state aid decisions of one mid-sized and five large cross-border European banks

	Balance sheet total (€ bn)						Burden-sharing		Business reduction		
	2008	2009	2010	2011	2012	2013	Remuner-ation	Coupon	Core market	Balance sheet (%)	Bans
Standard rule							-/+	(-)	(-)	50	(-)
Commerzbank	625	844	754	662	636	550	+	+/-	-	>45	++
Dexia	651	578	567	413	357	223	+	-	+	>35	++
ING	1332	1164	1247	1279	1169	1081	+	-	+	>45	++
KBC	355	324	321	285	257	241	+	+	+/-	<20	+
Lloyds (£)	436	1027	992	971	925	847	+	+	+	<20	+
RBS (£)	2402	1696	1454	1507	1312	1028	+	+/-	+	>25	+

Data sources: Nicola Pesaresi and DG Competition, European Commission; European Commission, *State Aid Monitor*; and banks annual reports.

Box 3. Main points of state aid decisions affecting five large cross-border banks and one mid-sized bank

Commerzbank

- *State aid:* Recapitalisation worth €8.2 billion and a guarantee framework for securities worth up to €15 billion (October 2008), additional equity capital totalling €10 billion (January 2009)
- Internal headcount reduction and restructuring/downsizing programme (45% reduction of balance sheet)
- Divestment of Eurohypo by 2014 at the latest
- Reduction of investment banking operations and divestment of some entities (Kleinwort Benson)
- Reduced market presence in Central and Eastern Europe
- Acquisition ban until April 2012
- Dividend ban (2008-09)
- Price leadership ban

Dexia

- *State aid:* €8.4 billion recapitalisation and guarantee or guaranteed liquidity assistance of €95-135 billion
- Domestic (life insurance business, retail branches, bond portfolio) and international (Crediop, RCB International, Dexia bank Slovakia, …) divestment programme
- 35% reduction in Dexia's balance sheet total by end-2014 compared to end-2008
- Reduction of short-term funding from 30% of total balance sheet in 2009 to 11% in 2014
- Reduction of operational costs by 15% by end-2012
- Dividend ban (until end-2011)
- Acquisition ban (until end 2011)
- Advertising restrictions
- Adherence to G-20 remuneration principles

ING

- *State aid:* Recapitalisation €10 billion and €12 billion of liquidity guarantees (October 2008), illiquid asset back-up facility covering 80% of a portfolio of $39 billion (January 2009)
- Internal headcount reduction and restructuring programme (45% balance sheet reduction)
- Divestment of several ING insurance brands and complete separation of banking and insurance by end 2013
- Divestment of ING Direct US (considered to be core by the group, but to be divested by 2013)
- Divestment of new company for Dutch retail financial market (composed of mortgage and consumer credit activities)

- Price leadership ban for the EU for certain retail and SME banking products for three year period maximum
- Acquisition ban for three-year period maximum

KBC

- *State aid*: Recapitalisation of €3.5 billion (December 2008), a second recapitalisation of another €3.5 billion (January 2009) and an asset relief measure on a portfolio containing CDOs (May 2009)
- Divestment of KBL Private Bank
- Divestment of non-core activities in Central and Eastern-Europe (Serbia, Slovenia and Russia)
- Divestment or scaling down a number of specialist investment banking activities, including most of the operations of the subsidiary, KBC Financial Products
- Sale of several complementary distribution channels in Belgium
- Focus on six home markets in bank-insurance for retail and SMEs in Belgium and five countries in Central and Eastern Europe, namely the Czech Republic, Slovakia, Hungary, Poland and Bulgaria
- Scaling back a large proportion of loan portfolios outside home markets
- Dividend, acquisition and price leadership ban

Lloyds

- *State aid*: £17 billion recapitalisation (January 2009) and £5.9 billion (November 2009)
- Asset reduction programme (£181 billion by end-2014)
- Divestment programme of some brands (including TSB)
- Divestment of 600 branches in England and Wales (corresponding to 4.6% market of the current account market), and behavioural constraints
- Acquisition ban
- dividend ban

Royal Bank of Scotland

- *State aid*: £15 billion recapitalisation and £5 billion preference shares (October 2008), converted into ordinary shares in January 2009. Further injection of £25.5 billion in November 2009, giving the state a total stake of 84%
- Internal headcount reduction and restructuring programme
- Large divestment programme (including RBS Insurance)
- Divestment of foreign participations (e.g. Bank of China)
- Sales corresponding to 25-30% of balance sheet
- 14% ceiling in SME market

Source: State Aid Register, DG Competition, European Commission.

Given that each of these banks operate with different business models and in different circumstances, it is obvious that the outcome of these state aid decisions is 'tailor-made'. Commerzbank and RBS had just engaged in a large acquisition before the crisis erupted (Dresdner Bank, respectively ABN AMRO's wholesale banking unit), leading to substantial adjustments. However, the large losses were in the RBS case covered by a large recapitalisation by the British state, in the case of Commerzbank through a subordinated debt subscription and more limited capital injection by the German federal republic. In ING's case, the crisis forced it to rethink its business model, reducing complexity and to focus on its core business: banking. KBC had to reduce its number of home markets and divest its private banking, but was not asked to divest insurance; Lloyds substantially reduced its dominance in the UK market, after the forced acquisition of HBOS.

The degree of requested balance sheet reduction differed considerably: from less than 20% in KBC, to 45% in ING and Commerzbank. The argumentation for the large-scale reduction in ING was that the aid amounted to more than 2% of risk-weighted assets, but this was also the case for KBC and Lloyds, which were less heavily sanctioned. According to the Commission, the latter two cases were satisfactory on behavioural constraints, hence the balance sheet reduction was lower. From what can be observed until end-2012, the outcome of the balance sheet reduction led to mixed results.

On several occasions, the Commission mentions that it will use the restructuring plans to increase competition in the local retail banking markets. The concentration in retail financial markets in the smaller member states is a well-known problem, which the Commission's competition policy directorate addressed in a 2007 inquiry (European Commission, 2007). Although overall the inquiry concluded that retail banking markets in the EU were only moderately concentrated, they were highly concentrated in Finland, the Netherlands, Belgium and Sweden. Increasing competition in the home market is explicitly mentioned in the decisions on ING, KBC and Lloyds as reason for requiring certain divestments.[64] On the other hand, the European Commission's state aid unit has mandated the divestment of foreign entities of state aided banks,

---

[64] Explicitly mentioned in the press releases on ING and KBC, European Commission, 18 November 2009.

and to focus on some core markets, which reduces competition at EU level. This has led to the criticism that it was acting contrary to its own objectives.

It could be argued that the Commission was measuring competition at national level, not at European level. The French refinancing scheme, agreed in October 2008, was cleared the same month by the Commission, who judged that the scheme was an appropriate, necessary and proportionate means of remedying a serious disturbance in the French economy. The Commission authorised it as it gave non-discriminatory access for all banks authorised in France, including the subsidiaries of foreign groups; it included a pricing mechanism that covered the funding costs of the scheme and ensured a fair contribution by the beneficiary banks, and it had appropriate safeguards against abuse of the scheme.

The same happened with the recapitalisation scheme, which was authorised by the European Commission on the same grounds. Under the SPPE (Société de Prises de Participation de l'Etat) structure, the state invested in securities issued by the beneficiary banks. These securities took the form of hybrid capital instruments (subordinated debt securities classified as non-core Tier 1 capital) and were remunerated at a fixed rate for the first five years and at a variable rate thereafter. The remuneration, which averaged about 8%, reflected the degree of solvency of each beneficiary bank via a credit default swap (CDS) component, whereby remuneration is modulated according to the risk of default. All large French banks benefited from the scheme, but it did not lead to any specific demands on the banks involved.[65] Only one French bank was the subject of an individual state aid procedure, the Banque Populaire/Caisse d'Épargne, which benefited from €2.45 billion government aid, on top of that already granted under the French scheme. But also that case was cleared by the European Commission without further restructuring demands.[66] This compares to 12 individual bank cases in Germany, some of which are still under in-depth investigation, and much deeper restructuring demands.

---

[65] See cases 613/2008 (recap) and 548/2008 (refinancing) in the European Commission's state aid register.

[66] Case N249/2009.

It should thus come as no surprise that some states felt unjustly treated, leading to criticism of arbitrariness and inflexibility in the decisions. In January 2010, ING lodged an appeal with the European Court of Justice against specific elements of the EC's Decision of 18 November 2009. ING objected to the price leadership restrictions and the proportionality of the restructuring requirements demanded by the European Commission. In addition, the Commission judged that the early repayment by ING to the Dutch state of the first tranche of the subordinated debt as additional state aid of approximately €2 billion. Both ING and the Dutch state contested this element of the Decision.[67] The Commission argued that early repayment would distort the level playing field again. In an historic court case, the Court of Justice of the European Union judged that renegotiation of the reimbursement conditions may not necessarily amount to additional state aid, arguing that a private investor would have done the same.[68]

8.7   State aid cases during the sovereign crisis

The highest profile cases in the second phase of the crisis were undoubtedly the Spanish savings banks, although the Greek, Cypriot and Irish cases should also be discussed. But the crisis continued to affect other countries as well, such as Denmark, the Netherlands, Belgium or Germany. The exceptional situation in the financial sector continued in many countries until well into 2013, also in core countries such as Denmark and Germany.

The **Spanish savings banks** cases, agreed upon in November 2012, ended a 2-year long process of increasing concerns about the health of the Spanish banking sector, but was also the first state aid case where a bail-in was applied on a large scale, to preferred stock (*preferentes*) and subordinated debt holders, and where burden-sharing was enforced. Of the estimated €59 billion needed to recapitalise the financial sector in Spain, about €12.7 billion was

---

[67] See ING 2009 Annual Report, p. 12.

[68] Judgement of the ECJ, 2 March 2012, Cases T-29/10 and T-33/10. See also Clifford Chance (2012), ING's landmark victory brightens the outlook for State aid recipients, Client Briefing, March.

raised though bail-ins, compared to €38.8 billion public money, lent to Spain by the European Stability Mechanism (ESM).[69] Notwithstanding this sum, the losses in the Spanish savings banks were enormous, with the direct capital support (not including impaired asset measures or state guarantees) to the banks from the beginning of the crisis amounting to €61.9 billion, or 6.1% of 2013 GDP. Spain also created a bad bank scheme in November 2012, the SAREB, to which a substantial part of the assets of the restructured banks were transferred. It was decided that the average value of the assets transferred to the bad bank should be 63.1%. In early 2013, SAREB had more than €50 billion in assets (compared to a gross value of over €100 billion).

Box 4. Main points of state aid decisions affecting the Spanish savings banks

BFA-Bankia

- *State aid*: In form of direct capital injections of €22.4 bn, and capital relief and impaired asset measures amounting to up to €13.8 billion (or in total 22% of its RWA as of 31 December 2011), in addition to the State guarantees on senior unsecured debt for a total of €53.9 billion.
- Haircut of 38% for holders of preferred stock and 36% for subordinated debt
- Reduction of branch network and headcount
- Decrease its existing geographical footprint
- Remuneration control
- Coupon ban
- Marketing and acquisition ban

Catalunya Banc

- *State aid*: In form of capital injections €12.05 billion and impaired asset measures up to €1.6 billion (32.3% of RWA), in addition to guarantees on €10.76 billion assets.
- Haircut of 61% for holders of preferred stock and 40% for perpetual subordinated debt
- Reduction of branch network and headcount
- Focus on core region and businesses

---

[69] IMF (2013), Spain: Financial Sector Reform—Third Progress Report, July.

Nova Caixa Galicia
- *State aid*: Capital injections totalling €9.1 billion and guarantees up to €7.5 billion on bonds issued under the Spanish guarantee scheme
- Haircut of 43% for holders of preferred stock and 40% for subordinated debt
- Focus on core region and businesses, non-core divestments
- Marketing and acquisition ban

Sources: State Aid Register, DG Comp, European Commission.

Table 10. State aid decision of the main Spanish savings banks

	Balance sheet total (€ bn)				Burden-sharing			Behavioural commitments		
	2010	2011	2012	2013	Remun eration	Coupon ban	Bail-in pref./ sub debt	Core market	Balance sheet (%)	Bans
Standard rule					-/+	(-)		(-)	50	(-)
BFA Bankia	n.a.	298	278	251	++	+	38% - 36%	+	>40	++
Catalunya Banca	77	77	74	63	+	-	61% - 40%	+	>20	++
Nova Caixa Galicia	67	72	60	53	+	-	43% - 40%	+	>30	++

Source: Aid Register, DG Competition, European Commission; IMF (2013) and bank annual reports.

Ireland was the EU country that started the bail-outs with huge bank support measures in September 2008, but continued to struggle throughout the sovereign crisis. Expressed as a % of GDP, the support for the financial sector was highest in Ireland of all EU countries. All local banks were affected, and Ireland's debt to GDP also doubled as a result of the financial crisis, raising questions about the sustainability of its public finances.

The highest profile case was Anglo-Irish Bank, which received a cumulated capital injection of €29.3 billion, upon a total balance sheet of €72 billion in 2010 (€101 billion at the end of 2008), an even higher absolute amount than Bankia. Anglo-Irish was a 'monoline' bank specialising in commercial real estate lending in three core markets: Ireland, the United Kingdom and the United States, three markets that faced huge declines during the crisis. However, with more than 30% aid to total balance sheet, or 18% of the Irish 2012 GDP, one could wonder whether this 'limits the restructuring costs and the amount of State aid to the minimum necessary', and whether the bank had to be bail-out for systemic reasons. The Commission considered, however, that an immediate liquidation would be more costly than an orderly resolution and would require more state aid.[70]

The two largest banks, Allied Irish banks, and Bank of Ireland, also received substantial capital injections, €13.1 billion respectively €5.2 billion, apart from impaired asset measures and liability guarantees. The capital support to these three banks alone adds up to 29% of the Irish 2012 GDP.

Greece had no individual bank state aid cases in the first stage of the financial crisis, but a general guarantee and recapitalisation fund (HFSF) that had been approved from November 2008 onwards. With the start of the sovereign crisis, the huge decline in economic activity, and the deposit flight, the needs grew exponentially, and the HFSF was endowed with €50 billion of the EU money to save Greece from default. The four large Greek banks Alpha Bank, EFG Eurobank, Piraeus Bank and National Bank of Greece received total capital support amounting to €18 billion. After the 2015 crisis, a new package of capital support for the Greek banks was approved by the European Council.

8.8 Conclusions

The containment of the financial and sovereign crisis was the result of a vast comprehensive effort by governments, central banks and international authorities. Measures to stabilise the financial sector and support the economy taken at EU and national levels have benefited all financial players and economic actors. But some financial institutions or sectors were in need of much more substantial support than others.

The direct state support happened in a very disparate and non-coordinated matter, however, in contrast to what the Eurogroup meeting of 12 October 2008 had affirmed. Many member states chose to call upon a national scheme to support the entire

---

[70] Commission Decision of 29.06.2011 on state aid, No SA.32504 (2011/N) and C 11/2010 (ex N 667/2009).

financial sector, but the schemes varied widely in scale and scope. In other cases, states provided support to individual banks, or through a combination of both. But the quality of sovereign guarantees and aid differed significantly, thus favouring 'weak' borrowers with a 'strong' sovereign backing, or disadvantaging 'strong' borrowers with a 'weak' sovereign backing. To break the doom-loop between banks and their sovereigns the European Council agreed on the creation of a Banking Union in June 2012.

Seen in hindsight, comprehensive national support *schemes* raised much less of a competition policy problem, as they provided support for the whole banking sector in a certain country.[71] The French scheme was a case in point, since it was imposed on all the large banks, and rapidly got the blessing of the EU, as it was non-discriminatory. In other countries, the problem with some banks was much more acute, and required direct state support, often in addition to a national scheme. The end-result is that some banks ended up in a tight restructuring and downsizing plan imposed by the European Commission, whereas others have fared almost unaffected. A direct consequence of these differences in national policies is that the banking landscape emerged entirely reshaped after the crisis.

The question whether the single market was maintained seems almost rhetorical in this perspective. Banking started on a much more uneven playing field after the crisis than before. To some extent, there is only the bank and its management to blame. But national policy-makers could also be criticised for their limited knowledge of the EU's state aid rules, for their incapacity to put together a comprehensive support plan and for not having reacted rapidly enough. The renewed legislative and supervisory framework, including the recovery and resolution framework, must ensure that the markets become more European again.

---

[71] See also Boughdene et al. (2010), who came to the same conclusion in an overview regarding asset relief measures in the EU.

References

Ayadi, R., W.P. De Groen and P. Thyri (2015), "State Aid to Banks and Credit for SMEs: Is there a need for Conditionality?", European Parliament, Study for the Economics and Monetary Affairs Committee, February.

Boudghene, Y., S. Maes and M. Scheicher (2010), "Asset Relief Measures in the EU – Overview and Issues" (available at SSRN: http://ssrn.com/abstract=1677310).

CEPR (2010), "Bailing out the Banks: Reconciling Stability and Competition", Centre for Economic Policy Research, London.

De Meester, B. (2010), "The Global Financial Crisis and Government Support for Banks: What Role for the GATS?", *Journal of International Economic Law*, Vol. 13, No. 1, pp. 42-43.

European Central Bank (2009), "National Rescue Measures in Response to the Current Financial Crisis", July.

_____ (2010), "Financial Integration in Europe, April.

European Commission (2007), Sector Inquiry under Article 17 of Regulation (EC) No 1/2003 on retail banking (Final Report), January (http://eur-lex.europa.eu/LexUriServ/site/en/com/2007/com2007_0033en01.pdf).

_____ (2009a), "Economic Crisis in Europe: Causes, Consequences and Responses", European Economy, September.

_____ (2009b), DG Competition's review of guarantee and recapitalisation schemes in the financial sector in the current crisis, August.

_____ (2010), State aid scoreboard (spring 2010), Report from the European Commission, COM(2010)255.

_____ (2011), The effects of temporary State aid rules adopted in the context of the financial and economic crisis, Staff Working Papers, October, SEC(2011)1126.

_____ (2013), State Aid Scoreboard, December.

Grande, M. (1999), "Possible decentralisation of state aid control in the banking sector", conference speech, Florence, June.

International Monetary Fund (2009), "Navigating the financial challenges ahead", Global Financial Stability Report, Washington, D.C., October.

_____ (2010), "Crisis Management and Resolution for a European Banking System", Working Paper, Washington, D.C., March.

_____ (2013), "Spain: Financial Sector Reform — Third Progress Report", Washington, D.C., July.

Lannoo, K., A. Sutton and C. Napoli (2010), *Bank State Aid in the Financial Crisis: Fragmentation or level playing field*, CEPS Task Force Report, Centre for European Policy Studies, Brussels, October.

Levy, A. and S. Schich (2010), "The Design of Government Guarantees for Bank Bonds: Lessons from the Recent Financial Crisis", *Financial Market Trends* (OECD Journal), No. 1.

Soltesz, U. and C. von Kockritz (2010), "From State Aid Control to Regulation of the European Banking System – DG Comp and the Restructuring of Banks", *European Competition Journal*, Vol. 6, No. 1, April.

Speyer, B. (2010), "The case for a Financial Sector Stabilisation Fund", *Monitor*, No. 73, Deutsche Bank Research.

9. CONCLUSIONS: SAFE TO BANK?

The financial and economic crisis will remain in the public memory for at least a generation to come, and concerns about the safety and soundness of the financial system will haunt policy-makers and the public alike. The vast array of regulatory reforms, described in this book, are largely a reaction to the past crisis, critics argue, and there is no assurance they can avoid or withstand the next one. The whole body of global financial regulatory reform has not been based on a clear design, but rather grew progressively, starting after the Great Depression in the 1930s and evolving in different ways across the various countries affected. A wave of liberalisation started in the 1970s, which in the EU context was later encapsulated in the single market programme, which harmonised the basic prudential standards for banking and finance. A second wave followed in the late 1990s, with the start of the Basel II discussions, which in the EU coincided with the launch of monetary union. But the financial crisis abruptly stopped this process and reinstated old recipes from the 1930s on the menu.

While not perfect, we would argue that the EU, in close cooperation with the G-20, managed to push through a well-designed process of regulatory reform in a limited period of time. Following its determination to subject "all systemically important financial institutions, markets and instruments ... to an appropriate degree of regulation and oversight," the G-20 adopted a clear programme for financial sector re-regulation. In certain areas, such as oversight of rating agents, hedge funds and derivatives markets, these elements had already been on the agenda of policy-makers – but without consensus on the way to act. For other areas, such as the resolution of banks, an entirely new framework was put in place, with a global approach for the bail-in of debt-holders, in case banks fail to meet minimum thresholds for capital. In the EU specifically, the crisis made policy-makers realise the need for stronger centralisation of supervision, which culminated in the

Banking Union proposals, with a single supervisor and a single resolution authority – a major step forward.

The paramount question remains implementation and enforcement. A vast array of new measures have been put in place, creating the formidable challenge for policy-makers and supervisors of applying them consistently, and for banks and operators of complying with them. In the EU in particular, because of the single market and the need for a single rulebook, the G-20 commitments were implemented through a long list of regulations and directives, and an even longer list of secondary legislation (implementing regulatory and technical standards). For the eurozone and the countries that opt in to the SSM, the expertise of the ECB should be a source of reassurance, but the challenge of bringing European banking markets in line with a single template is huge. For large eurozone banks, the change from the comfort of communicating with the national administration in the capital to dealing with one distant European supervisor for the entire group in Frankfurt is more profound than the start of monetary union, which unified monetary policy but left its execution, i.e. the liquidity-providing operations, decentralised.

Once fully in place, the resolution and deposit guarantee schemes framework should provide a substantial buffer for coping with future banking crises. This should be seen in combination with all the steps that have been taken in recent years to make banks safer and more resilient to crises, but also to allow banks to fail, if necessary, in an organised way. The debate surrounding the presumed lack of a fiscal backstop needs to be qualified, as it does not sufficiently take into account all the layers of defence that exist to make the financial system more resilient.

The first layer of defence is a much plumper cushion for absorbing losses, composed of a higher level of capital, under a tighter definition, as shown in Table 11. In addition, authorities can request macro-prudential, systemic and institution-specific capital buffers in different forms, such as for globally systemically important institutions. As capital is measured on a risk-weighted basis, this should be complemented from 2018 onwards with a minimum leverage ratio. As soon as a bank falls below the 8% capital ratio, it will be requested by the resolution authorities to return to that level through an asset sale or rights issue, or proceed with a bail-in, which should happen smoothly if it is of a limited magnitude.

The question remains of how a crisis in a large bank or region will be dealt with, and whether the funds in place are sufficient to cope with it. These matters are even more urgent given the transition period between now and 2024, during which time the deposit insurance and resolution funds will not yet be fully funded. A large bail-in for a bank in excess of €1 trillion in assets will not take place without having effects on global capital markets. This step will most likely be taken in tandem with the disposal of certain entities of the group, whereby the resolution and/or the deposit insurance fund will be called upon, causing further challenges for global coordination. A €55 billion resolution fund for the eurozone is very small indeed, compared to the sums the US provided under TARP (Troubled Asset Relief Program, initially set at $700 billion) or to AIG in 2008, or to the €25 billion needed to recapitalise the Greek banks after the 2015 crisis. Emergency lending assistance (ELA) may also be used as a temporary solution, but even within the Eurozone, this is provided by the national central bank. It remains to be seen how a single approach will be applied in these circumstances.

Table 11. Layers of defence for bank crisis

	What minimum?	**Where and when?**	**Before**
Capital	4.5% CET1, 6% incl. additional Tier 1 capital, and 8% incl. Tier 2 capital, risk-weighted	Global, EU and EEA	4% Tier 1 upon looser definition of capital, 8% total capital, risk-weighted
Capital add-ons and macro-prudential buffer	G-SIBs (up to +3.5% CET1), O-SIIs (up to +2% CET1) Capital Conservation buffer (+2.5% CET1) Countercyclical capital buffer (up to +2.5% CET1) Systemic risk buffer (0%-3%-5% CET1)	EU and EEA	Only in a few member states

Leverage ratio	3%, non-risk-weighted	Global, EU and EEA expected from 2018 onwards	Not in EU
Bail-in	Minimum 8% of total liabilities and own funds	EU and EEA, from 2016 onwards	Non-existent
Deposit Guarantee Schemes	Pre-funding at 0.8% of covered deposits, max coverage €100,000 per depositor per bank	EU and EEA, to be fully in place in 2024 at the latest	Only €18.6 billion (2011) in DGS funds in the EU
Resolution Fund	1% of the amount of covered deposits; covering max 5% of liabilities in case of resolution	EU and EEA, to be fully in place in 2024 at the latest	Non-existent
Single Resolution Fund	Pre-funding at 1% of covered deposits	EMU and opt-ins, to be fully in place in 2024 at the latest	Non-existent
European Stability Mechanism	€55 billion direct recap facility	EMU, since June 2014	Non-existent

The ultimate backstop for the eurozone is the European Stability Mechanism, when a bank has no clear national parent or a weak sovereign, but the amount allocated for the recapitalisation facility remains low. Since the ESM is state-funded, however, it could be significantly increased, if necessary. But in the latter case, the decision will need to be taken by unanimous agreement by all, or almost all ESM members. The most recent episodes in the Greek crisis has shown that unanimity would not be easy to obtain.

The challenge for the years to come is to extend the logic of the SSM, and Banking Union in general, to other parts of the financial system, where needed, and eventually to make the necessary changes to the supervisory architecture. The EU Treaty article that passed banking supervision to the ECB was an easy solution to centralising supervision and gave a clear sign to the markets that the lessons of the past had been heeded. In the longer term, the question needs to remain on the agenda of whether this is the best solution or whether it would be preferable to separate supervision from monetary policy in an altogether different European institution. The specific European supervisory needs of the insurance sector, capital markets and financial infrastructures also require close monitoring, more cooperation and possibly changes to the EU Treaty. So far, member states have been reluctant to follow the logic of Banking Union for the supervision of market infrastructures such as CSDs or CCPs, which does not make sense. A more rational division of labour between the EBA and the ECB should also be on the agenda.

Another priority is the allocation of macro-prudential supervisory tasks that will require further streamlining. In the current set-up, they remain scattered across different entities, both national and European, which does not facilitate coordinated action. The CRD IV formally maintained important macro-prudential powers and the possibility to impose specific measures, such as capital buffers, at the national level. Macro-prudential coordination is undertaken by the ESRB within the ECB for the whole of the EU, but this body can only act in an advisory capacity, while the SSM has the capacity to overrule national measures for eurozone banks and countries that have opted-in.

The complexity of rules and rulemaking is a major issue of concern and one that has spiralled out of control. Firstly, to fulfil the promise of a single rulebook, the primary legislation has become very complex and detailed. Secondly, much reliance is placed on secondary legislation in regulatory and technical standards in hundreds of separate pieces of legislation, which often fall outside parliamentary control. Remembering the adage that "complexity is the road towards capture", this does not necessarily facilitate good oversight; on the contrary. Supervisors and banks may be bogged down in details and lose sight of the overall picture.

Hence, even if the SSM started in November 2014, creating an integrated regulatory and supervisory framework will remain a work in progress.

ANNEX: OVERVIEW OF BANKING AND FINANCE LEGISLATION

- **Banking**

Single Supervisory Mechanism (SSM)

Council Regulation (EU) No 1024/2013 of 15 October 2013 conferring specific tasks on the European Central Bank concerning policies relating to the prudential supervision of credit institutions

Single Resolution Mechanism (SRM)

Regulation (EU) No 806/2014 of the European Parliament and of the Council of 15 July 2014 establishing uniform rules and a uniform procedure for the resolution of credit institutions and certain investment firms in the framework of a Single Resolution Mechanism and a Single Resolution Fund

Council implementing Regulation (EU) 2015/81 of 19 December 2014 specifying uniform conditions of application of Regulation (EU) No 806/2014 with regard to ex ante contributions to the Single Resolution Fund

Bank Recovery and Resolution Directive (BRRD)

Directive 2014/59/EU of the European Parliament and of the Council of 15 May 2014 establishing a framework for the recovery and resolution of credit institutions and investment firms

Deposit Guarantee Schemes Directive (DGSD)

Directive 2014/49/EU of the European Parliament and of the Council of 16 April 2014 on deposit guarantee schemes

Capital Requirements Directive (CRD IV)

Directive 2013/36/EU of the European Parliament and of the Council of 26 June 2013 on access to the activity of credit institutions and the prudential supervision of credit institutions and investment firms

Capital Requirements Regulation (CRR)

Regulation (EU) No 575/2013 of the European Parliament and of the Council of 26 June 2013 on prudential requirements for credit institutions and investment firms

- ## Securities markets and investment firms

Markets in Financial Instruments Regulation (MIFiR)

Regulation (EU) 600/2014 of the European Parliament and of the Council of 15 May 2014 on markets in financial instruments

Markets in Financial Instruments Directive (MiFID II)

Directive 2014/65/EU of the European Parliament and of the Council of 15 May 2014 on markets in financial instruments

Market Abuse Regulation (MAR)

Regulation (EU) No 596/2014 of the European Parliament and of the Council of 16 April 2014 on market abuse

Market Abuse Directive (MAD II)

Directive 2014/57/EU of the European Parliament and of the Council of 16 April 2014 on criminal sanctions for market abuse

Short Selling Regulation (SSR)

Regulation (EU) No 236/2012 of the European Parliament and of the Council of 14 March 2012 on short selling and certain aspects of credit default swaps

TD

Directive 2013/50/EU of the European Parliament and of the Council of 22 October 2013 amending Directive 2004/109/EC of the European Parliament and of the Council on the harmonisation of transparency requirements in relation to information about issuers whose securities are admitted to trading on a regulated market

Credit Rating Agency Regulation (CRAR)

Regulation (EU) No 462/2013 of the European Parliament and of the Council of 21 May 2013 amending Regulation (EC) No 1060/2009 on credit rating agencies

- ## Investment funds and managers

Undertakings for Collective Investment in Transferable Securities (UCITS V)

Directive 2014/91/EU of the European Parliament and of the Council of 23 July 2014 on the coordination of laws, regulations and administrative provisions relating to undertakings for collective investment in transferable securities as regards depositary functions, remuneration policies and sanctions

Alternative Investment Fund Managers Directive (AIFMD)

Directive 2011/61/EU of the European Parliament and of the Council of 8 June 2011 on Alternative Investment Fund Managers

European Venture Capital Funds (EuVECA)

Regulation (EU) No 345/2013 of the European Parliament and of the Council of 17 April 2013 on European venture capital funds

European Social Entrepreneurship Funds (EuSEF)

Regulation (EU) No 346/2013 of the European Parliament and of the Council of 17 April 2013 on European social entrepreneurship funds

European long-term investment funds (ELTIF)

Regulation (EU) 2015/760 of the European Parliament and of the Council of 29 April 2015 on European long-term investment funds

Packaged Retail and Insurance-based Investment Products (PRIPS)

Regulation (EU) No 1286/2014 of the European Parliament and of the Council of 26 November 2014 on key information documents for packaged retail and insurance-based investment products

- ## Market infrastructure

European Market Infrastructure Regulation (EMIR)

Regulation (EU) No 648/2012 of the European Parliament and of the Council of 4 July 2012 on OTC derivatives, central counterparties and trade repositories

Central Securities Depositories Regulation (CSDR)

Regulation (EU) No 909/2014 of the European Parliament and of the Council of 23 July 2014 on improving securities settlement in the European Union and on central securities depositories

Settlement finality in payment and securities settlement system Directive (SFD)

Directive 2009/44/EC of the European Parliament and of the Council of 6 May 2009 amending Directive 98/26/EC on settlement finality in payment and securities settlement systems and Directive 2002/47/EC on financial collateral arrangements as regards linked systems and credit claims

INDEX